VW GOLF

MK I–IV

RICHARD COPPING

Acknowledgements

The author and publisher would like to thank Volkswagen AG for permission to use both copyright press images and brochure photography throughout.

The author would like to thank fellow VW enthusiasts Brian Screaton and Keith Bolton for the interest they have shown as the research and writing process for this book took place.

First published 2023

Amberley Publishing
The Hill, Stroud,
Gloucestershire, GL5 4EP

www.amberley-books.com

ISBN: 978 1 3981 1337 4 (print)
ISBN: 978 1 3981 1338 1 (ebook)

British Library Cataloguing in Publication Data.
A catalogue record for this book is available from the British Library.

Typeset in 10pt on 13pt Celeste.
Typesetting by SJmagic DESIGN SERVICES, India.
Printed in the UK.

Contents

1968–1974: From Air to Water Cooling – A Bumpy Transition

The end of a golden era

On 12 April 1968 the well-oiled cogs of the fourth – or on occasion third – largest automobile manufacturer in the world ground to a temporary halt following the announcement of the death of its leader, Heinz Nordhoff, after twenty years at the helm. It was this giant of the industry who had virtually single-handedly transformed the ownerless, one-time Nazi factory at Wolfsburg from an unprofitable badly bomb-damaged wreck producing 7,000 cars per annum (providing it didn't rain too much) into the organisation VW had become with tentacles in the vast majority of countries across the world.

Nordhoff had achieved what he did on the back of the People's Car, the volks wagen, a low-cost sedan designed by Ferdinand Porsche in the 1930s for use by Germans previously restricted by financial constraints to bicycles, or at best a motorbike. Throughout the 1950s

Successors to the Beetle - one model and four facelifts, or four different cars allocated a name meaning gulfstream?

This press image allows a glimpse of the four generations of the GTi, Volkswagen's ground-breaking hot-hatch – and from 1976 a different and very successful direction in which to travel.

and into the 1960s, however much cash Nordhoff invested in expansion demand for the car we know as the Beetle outstripped supply. A second string to Nordhoff's bow was the multi-use, people-carrying or load-lugging Transporter, a vehicle initially manufactured at Wolfsburg, but from 1956 the occupant of a purpose-built factory at Hanover. Production of the niche market Cabriolet version of the Beetle and the same car with a sporty body, the Karmann Ghia, was delegated to the coachbuilder's Karmann, but in the 1960s Nordhoff found room for a larger family saloon – the VW 1500. At the time of his death, production of a still larger saloon and attendant 'variant' (estate car) was only months away.

In 1965 production of the Beetle passed the million units produced in a twelve-month period hurdle for the first time. It did so again the following year and was set to do so again in the year of Nordhoff's death. In the summer of 1967 a brand new incarnation of the Transporter was launched, while the Beetle underwent sufficient visible/practical changes for the Wolfsburg marketing team to describe the '68 model as the 'New' Beetle. Sustained profitability amid ongoing expansion was a hallmark of the Nordhoff regime.

Beware the press and politicians

Nordhoff's unprecedented policy of continual improvement rather than the industry standard of replacing a model with another every few years – a policy of built-in obsolescence according to the Director General – stood him in good stead throughout

5 August 1955. Heinz Nordhoff (centre) is pictured alongside the millionth Beetle to be produced at Wolfsburg. Nordhoff was the man who took Volkswagen from a bombed-out factory producing a trickle of cars at unknown costs to the third largest manufacturer in the world after Ford and General Motors.

the 1950s. However, as the 1960s matured sectors of the automotive press began to make sufficient noise for Nordhoff to instruct that the numerous would-be Beetle replacement concept studies – numbering thirty-six surviving examples in total, ranging from the absurdity of a four-wheel drive twin through to a six-cylinder 2.0 litre, and each rejected by him – should be wheeled out to demonstrate that the manufacturer, largely through commissioning Porsche, had been far from idle.

Perhaps the Director General should have made more of his 1964 development centre, built next to the Mittelland canal and employing some 2,000 people, of the slightly later 1966 climatic wind tunnel (the largest such facility in Europe) and of the vast Ehra-Lessien test and development centre, started in 1966 in his quest to confirm that he would replace the Beetle if a suitable replacement of practical design and genuine improvements was forthcoming. Perhaps, more than anything else, in 1967 Nordhoff should have announced the creation of a special product planning committee that would develop plans for a future without both him and the Beetle.

Instead, either knowingly or by accident, Nordhoff became embroiled in politics. The latter months of 1966 saw Germany, like many other nations, tumble into a sharp recession. Ford, among others, simply made swathes of their workforce redundant, but Nordhoff chose a different course of action. He brought in a fairer system of short hours for all, but also introduced a special budget version of the Beetle, the Sparkäfer, which both kept the workforce occupied when demand was slack and helped to drive sales when money was tight. However, neither of these actions caused the politicians angst. It was Nordhoff's response to the new coalition government's initiatives in respect of transport that kindled their displeasure. Petrol taxes were raised, automobile insurance rates were allowed to spiral out of control and, crucially, the tax concession made if German workers drove their car to and from work was slashed in half. Nordhoff was openly scathing. Furious, the coalition government fought back, most notably through the bombastic Finance Minister, Franz-Josef Strauss, aided and abetted by sympathetic sections of the press. Bild declared that 'VW has been asleep', while Strauss accused Nordhoff of building up vast financial reserves at the expense of moving forward, not to mention producing an outdated car lacking modern creature comforts.

The recession was short-lived but the consequences of it remained for Nordhoff. Taking into account that Volkswagen was essentially a state-owned company, that in January 1968 the Director General was four years past the customary retirement age, and sadly that in July 1967 he suffered heart failure necessitating long periods of absence from Wolfsburg for the rest of the year, in crude terms both his own and the Beetle's future was signed and sealed. While those acting on behalf of the politicians didn't attempt to force Nordhoff to retire immediately, they did ensure that his potential successor was one of their own and hostile as hostile can be to the Director General.

Sadly, Nordhoff didn't live to see his retirement. On 15 March 1968, following a dash to Baden-Baden to make yet another rallying speech, Nordhoff collapsed. He died in Wolfsburg hospital just under a calendar month later.

The mercifully brief, but damaging, reign of Kurt Lotz

While it is conceivable that eventually there may have been a car made by Volkswagen given the name Golf, if it had been the work of Lotz's regime, it would have been a product of confused thinking, insipid design characteristics and dubiously niche and costly mechanical prowess.

Although it would be unfair to argue convincingly that Lotz simply lacked business experience, his expertise was totally divorced from the art of motor manufacturing. His appointment to succeed Nordhoff instead of the old Director General's long-term protégée was carefully engineered by a combination of politicians and supporting individuals who had already infiltrated the Wolfsburg giant.

From the start Lotz proved to be a malignant influence. Assiduously silent until after Nordhoff had gasped his last, within weeks of his death Lotz was openly criticising everything past. He declared that VW had been 'immovable under a single director for the past twenty years' and even less guardedly of Volkswagen's 'only chance of survival' being a new car. 'We had to move from monolith to a many-faceted product', he concluded.

That may or may not have been the case, but Lotz lacked the ability to effectively manage such a change. His achievements, if his actions may be so determined, confirm this. Instead of pumping large amounts of cash from Volkswagen's crammed bank vaults into

Kurt Lotz, Nordhoff's successor, was charged with changing everything that had made Volkswagen successful. He failed dismally and after three and a half years was relieved of his duties.

producing a Beetle replacement, Lotz spent unrealistic amounts on the creation of a new Beetle option, producing in the process the least popular incarnation to date, the 1302. This Beetle offered greater boot space (albeit stepped with two levels and therefore impractical and inconvenient) and offered allegedly improved drive and suspension thanks to the inclusion of MacPherson strut suspension at the car's front. The biggest downside was in terms of aesthetics, as the new 1302 looked front heavy, humped or even pregnant. Lacking conviction, Lotz sanctioned ongoing production of the traditional Beetle before approving development work that would add a further fusion of modernity – a curved windscreen and, horror of horrors, an all plastic moulded dash – in the mistaken belief that US infant health and safety legislation would demand a greater distance between driver and screen than the traditional Beetle and the 1302 offered.

In 1969 Volkswagen purchased the small and struggling German manufacturer NSU. Such a move was not unprecedented, as Nordhoff had bought the Daimler Benz subsidiary Auto Union GmbH four years previously. Nordhoff's reason for purchase was straightforward enough. First, he increased the VW Empire's product range overnight, while secondly he gained direct access to a whole generation of new engines. Lotz's principal reason for purchase was what he believed to be the acquisition of an 'oven-ready' Beetle replacement in the form of the almost ready to launch NSU K70. As if to prove the point, Lotz commanded a halt in the expansion programme of the research and development department. Apart from working on improvements to existing models, this was the body responsible for the design of new models and power-trains.

The absurdity of the notion of replacing the Beetle with the K70, even going to the extraordinary lengths of building a brand-new factory in Salzgitter for its production, can't be over-emphasised. In size and performance terms the K70 was closer to both the Audi 100 and the VW 411, the latter being the last model of the Nordhoff era, having been launched in the final months of 1968. Lotz's determination to manipulate the evolutionary story was apparent. To an eager automotive press and lines of would-be buyers, Lotz had introduced the VW 411 as 'no metal Adonis', while to pitch the K70's price below that of the Audi 100 he'd contented himself with a negligible profit of just 33DM per car sold. In one further attempt to prove the K70 a winner, Lotz had initially pushed its launch back – demanding a level of investment in perfecting the car that amounted to more than NSU's entire development programme.

The K70's dull and uncompromising three-box shape gave it a level of undesirable anonymity second to few if any others. Its appallingly bad drag coefficient of 0.51, which guaranteed an extreme thirst, its penchant for overheating issues, and its susceptibility to engine unreliability (in either 75 or 90 PS guise) quickly gave the K70 a reputation unlike that of any VW. Add to that premature rusting, which obviously wasn't known about in the early months, and a failure to penetrate the vital US market and here was the biggest flop in VW's history – one that could be fairly and squarely laid at Lotz's door.

Despite Lotz's curious decree that the development department would not be further expanded, at least an element of project work continued largely, though not exclusively, through the auspices of Porsche (as had been the case for many a year) and in no small part due to the cooperation between VW and the sports car manufacturer in bringing the mid-engined VW Porsche 914 to the market in the final months of 1969. Lotz's political masters, fed what they wanted to hear, believed they had a path to a Beetle replacement opening up. Hardly immersed in the detail, they were unaware that what Porsche was currently offering was both impractical and costly.

Known as EA266 (Entwicklungsauftrag Nummer 266, or Development Order 266), the car created by Porsche featured a chain-driven four-cylinder overhead-camshaft design water-cooled engine that rode flat on its side under the rear seat. Cooling air was dragged through one rear wheel arch and exited through the other. Otherwise the design was relatively conventional with lower wishbones and spring legs at the front and angled trailing arms at the rear. However, the location of the engine did allow a characteristic of both the VW1500/1600 and VW411/412 to filter through as EA266 was possessed of a boot at both the front and rear. The aim was to build 3,000 examples per day on launch, the date of which was anticipated at some point in 1973. The proposed engine location would have made EA266 both difficult to manufacture and, more noticeably, expensive to construct. Again, while it might be acceptable for a sports car to exhibit symptoms of engine noise, this was inappropriate in terms of small or for that matter, any other sized family saloon. The large cooling vents – essentially beneath the C pillars – might have foretold a story of smells, while those who saw the plans, or better still prototypes in the metal, couldn't help but notice how difficult it would be to access the engine for routine servicing. The practically minded predicted problems removing the rear seat with oily mechanics hands, while a primary characteristic of a test drive was of a vehicle tussling with cross winds.

Just as Lotz turned a blind eye to this catalogue of potential sales damaging issues, he also chose to ignore the undisputable fact that, in its form when according to one German newspaper fifty pre-production examples had been constructed in the metal, the EA266 could not be produced profitably.

The Beetle's less than satisfactory evolution in the Lotz years (not to mention a recall of over 200,000 1302s in 1970 thanks to a combination of poor fuel consumption and a wiring fault), his disastrous K70 initiative, and the damage he had deliberately inflicted on the VW 411 – not to mention the at-best dubious prolongation of the EA266 project – paled into insignificance when compared to his financial performance. In 1968 Volkswagenwerk AG generated a profit of 339 million Deutschmarks. This dropped to a tolerable 330 in 1969 and by a terrifying 140 million Deutschmarks to 190 million the following year. Come June 1971 and VW's latest annual general meeting, there was the very real likelihood of the appearance of red ink in the near future, although in reality the manufacturer scraped home at the end of the year, in the black by a mere 12 million Deutschmarks. However, by that point Lotz was gone, hastened out of the back door on 22 September by his one-time friends, a last-minute dash to Bonn and Chancellor Brandt armed with hastily dusted off prototype details proving fruitless. He was just three years and six months into his first five-year contract.

Rudolf Leiding: father of the Golf brand

Lotz's successor, Rudolf Leiding, was a very different animal from his predecessor. His involvement with VW had been even longer than Nordhoff's, as his first role was in 1945 when he was charged with repairing army vehicles. When Nordhoff secured his post as Director General, starting at Wolfsburg at the beginning of 1948, he picked Leiding to assist with the establishment of the first proper production line. From there, Leiding was despatched to the USA – where he was responsible for the establishment of the service network. In 1958 Leiding became the first manager of Volkswagen's new Kassel plant, where he stayed until 1965 before Nordhoff had another task for him. This was to pull the newly acquired and ailing Auto-Union into a semblance of a company owned by Volkswagen; his target the creation of a profitable operation. In his first year, Leiding had reduced production costs by 34 per cent, while by 1967 what we know as Audi was well and truly in the black.

Rudolph Leiding's tenure of office was short, but he successfully introduced a new generation of water-cooled front-wheel-drive cars to replace Nordhoff's air-cooled giants. The Golf proved a great success, but was destined to struggle in VW's biggest export market, the USA.

In July 1968, Leiding found himself on his way to Brazil. His task as head of the operation this time was to reverse the serious decline in sales experienced there, something he achieved with consummate ease. He also oversaw the introduction of new Volkswagen's specific to the South American market, while cranking up Beetle sales in a land where the old master was enjoying far from a last gap existence. His job done, Lotz called Leiding back to Germany and the newly merged Audi-NSU grouping to rationalise unit costs that were deemed excessive. Such was the nature of his meteoric rise, Lotz craftily offered him the position of his number two. Leiding wisely declined such a dubious honour.

Following Lotz's fall, Leiding took up the post as his successor, the third Director General in a period of just over four years. One of his first acts, within three weeks of taking up his appointment, was to cancel the EA266 project. Another was to reassess those neglected also-run avenues towards a Beetle replacement, unearthing one particular piece of work, the EA337, in the process, while a third was to pour enormous amounts of money into not just one but a full series of new cars. If the car eventually to be named the Golf was to be the true Beetle successor in Europe and key export markets, so too was the Audi-inspired Passat to be a replacement for the decade and more years old VW 1500/1600, plus the relatively new VW 411/12 series. Almost as a sideline, the elegant Karmann Ghia 'sports' car was also to be replaced by the equally attractive, but again more-or-less niche market, VW Scirocco. Possibly looked at by some as an afterthought, which it was most certainly not, the baby Audi 50 was rebadged as the Polo and in many ways, thanks to rampant inflation, oil crises and more, this was the true Beetle successor – a car that could readily accommodate both two adults and reasonably sized children, plus sufficient luggage to become an ideal means of transport for a younger family.

To put it mildly, the mid-1970s were trying times for manufacturers, politicians and whole nations, not just in Britain and Germany, but throughout the industrialised world. In October 1973 Egypt attacked Israel via the Suez Canal, while Syria did the same on the Golan Heights. The Arab–Israeli war proved to be a short-lived affair but its consequences were surprisingly lengthy. Arab oil producers announced an immediate cut in the supply of oil, a move which triggered both fuel rationing in the short term and offered longer-term consequences centring upon worldwide recession and unbridled inflation – not to mention politically activated, union-led worker discontent. At a time when adieu had yet to be bidden to the Beetle as a car manufactured in Germany, and new models including the Golf were either still in development or in a period of sales infancy, Leiding's Volkswagen suffered. That stalwart of past decades as well as the seventies, the Transporter, and the one model of Nordhoff's as yet not under threat from his successors, illustrates the dangerous ground occupied by the German manufacturing giant. In 1973 Volkswagen had produced 289,022 Transporters. The following year, that figure tumbled to 222,233, a drop of nearly 25 per cent – a level not improved upon during 1975. Significantly, a crucial part of that tumble related to Volkswagen's premier export market, the USA, until then a consistent filler of the German company's coffers thanks not just to the Transporter, but the Beetle as well.

Leiding's enormous spend to introduce the Golf et al could hardly have been more badly timed and sadly from an encouraging recorded profit of 86 million Deutschmarks in 1972, followed by a possibly unexpected 109 million the following year, Volkswagen tumbled into the chasm of a loss amounting to a staggering 555 million Deutschmarks in 1974. At least in his new cars Leiding had what he believed to be a way of easing the situation which threatened to drag Volkswagen under.

While domestic market sales tumbled by a recession-inspired 20 per cent in 1974, US figures were even more onerous, with a drop of a staggering 33 per cent recorded. To make matters worse still, US President Richard Nixon had devised and applied restrictions that favoured American-built cars by some 6 per cent. Union power had ensured that German labour received a wage increase of 11 per cent in 1973, the two moves going a great deal of the way to making Volkswagen's products prohibitively expensive. The ever-increasing burden of inflation dictated unwished for price increases, twice in the first six months of 1974 and again in August. Domestically, perhaps a smaller car, a rebadged Audi 50, would help. However, the US market was renowned for its large sedans and the Beetle held a unique position as a small car with such a quirky personality that the Americans took it to their hearts. A similar move there wouldn't be tolerated.

Leiding's solution was to reduce the price of US spec Volkswagens by building them locally. When he duly presented his ideas to the Supervisory Board in September 1974, the financial strategists reeled at the potential initial costs of such a move. When the unions got wind of it, they inevitably opposed the idea, frightened at the idea of creating foreign jobs at the possible risk of losing at least a percentage of their own.

Leiding felt his position was untenable and in December 1974 he requested that his contract be terminated on the grounds of ill health. The UK magazine *Autocar* was vehement in its criticism of Volkswagen for not giving him sufficient support to retain him as the creator of the business's future. 'There are few enough men who could have taken an ailing giant by the scruff of its neck and set it back on the right road, as Leiding did at Wolfsburg', they declared.

Leiding's successor, ex-Ford man Toni Schmücker, saw what he inherited blossom and grow. While VW made a loss of 145 million DM in 1975 as they cleared the backlog of Leiding's necessary expenditure, the following year a profit of 784 million DM was generated. Schmücker could sit back and bask in the glory of what was his immediate predecessor's work. Ironically in 1976, largely due to the dollar exchange rate, the wheels were set in motion to start building the Golf, or Rabbit as it was known in the US, locally.

Key to the Leiding story was who he chose to create the car seen as the Beetle's successor.

What's in a name?

To accompany the transition from air- to water-cooling, Volkswagen abandoned the traditional designations of Type 1, 2, 3 and 4 – the Beetle (virtually always a nickname), Transporter, VW 1500/1600 and the VW 411/12 respectively – in favour of allocating names associated with winds to each new vehicle entering the range.

First out of the next generation pod was the VW Passat. The German word translates as 'trade wind' or any easterly wind that helped mariners and particularly traders to sail around the world. Next to be released was the coach-built Karmann Ghia replacement, the 'sporty' option, a car which was named the Scirocco. The sirocco is a wind associated with the Mediterranean that originates in the Sahara. The third and most significant new VW

Jetta was the name given to the first generation Golf with a boot. The same name was destined to be used for all generations of booted saloon in the USA.

to be launched offered a decree of confusion to English-speaking nations, for it was named after the Gulf Stream, which when written in German is spelled 'golfstrom'. Hence, the VW Golf. The Gulf Stream is an ocean current that brings warmer water and air from the Gulf of Mexico, along the USA's east coast and across the Atlantic to the western coasts of Europe. The next arrival, the rebadged Audi 50 with a lower trim spec, was allocated the name Polo, for which read polar wind. Many assumed that this name continued a different trend established by the VW Golf.

Three further winds will be encountered over the course of this book, all of which are associated with the various editions of the booted version of the Golf. Most significant of these is the Jetta, the name given to the first- and second-generation cars with the Golf body and a boot. In the USA the name Jetta was retained for the third and fourth generation versions of such cars. However, in Europe the booted Golf became the Vento in Mk 3 days and then the Bora during the era of Mk 4. The Jetta name refers to the jet stream, while Vento is the word for non-specific winds in both Italian and Portuguese. The Bora label, on the other hand, is very precise, as the associated wind can be defined as a north to north-easterly winter phenomenon that blows intermittently over the Adriatic parts of Italy, Slovenia and Croatia, as well as areas of Greece, Russia, Turkey and Bulgaria.

The third generation booted Golf was known as the Vento in Europe and beyond, in an attempt to disassociate it from its slow-selling predecessors.

1974 –1983: Mk 1 - 'The Little Golf ABC – a Basic Course in Golf'

Leiding's speedy abandonment of the mid-engine concept as a Beetle replacement may have cost Volkswagen 250 million Deutschmarks, but it was the right choice. So too was his decision to dust off the dormant EA337 alternative. The man behind this development project had no link with either conservative, out-of-step Porsche, or to engineers, designers and stylists already working for VW.

Giorgetto Giugiaro had established his own design studio in 1967 on the back of his success as an employee of others, naming it Ital Styling and twelve months later renaming it Ital Design. Despite his youth – he was born in 1938 – or possibly because of it, he had been deluged with flattering reviews of his work to date.

To say that the thinking behind EA337 was spectacularly innovative is to adapt the truth. To argue that Giugiaro skilfully amalgamated ground-breaking and trending aspects of other works, while adding a soupcon of his own genius to make a near-perfect recipe for a Beetle successor, is more accurate. Britain's Mini of 1959 vintage, and a little later the Austin/Morris 1100, generated interest first in, and soon after demand for, transverse engine designs. The principal benefit of such an arrangement was more available room for passengers and luggage, a considerable plus point in the art of smaller car design. Taking the concept one stage further, Fiat had placed their gearboxes in-line with the engine, first in the Autobianchi Primula then in 1969 with the mainstream 128. The Mini also set the trend for cars with a wheel at each corner, rather than with overhangs, an arrangement offering both enhanced road holding and more cab and rear seat space. As long ago as the late 1950s, Austin had experimented with the hatchback idea, offering what they called the A40 Farina Countryman. This was marketed as an estate car but the proportions were wrong for such a vehicle. Under a decade later Renault's inventory of vehicles included three hatchback models, while Simca's 1100, introduced in 1967, was another car to exhibit both a hatchback and a transverse engine. Perhaps closest to EA337 in its make up was the Alfa Romeo Alfasud, a delightfully proportioned car which debuted in 1971, although Alfa had refused to countenance the hatchback the designer had originally incorporated. The similarities between the future Golf and the Alfasud are easily explained, as Ital Design was responsible for both designs.

Inevitably the Lotz regime had more-or-less left Giugiaro to his own devices, only specifying an ideal overall length and wheelbase, the latter for some reason being that of the Beetle. Considering that many cars are bought on the back of appealing styling, available space, creature comforts and possibly even available colours, rather than engine performance or reliability, gearing and braking abilities, not to mention suspension et al, Giugiaro was the ideal man for the job. At a time when run-of-the-mill designers appeared to be abandoning the angular for more rounded offerings, Giugiaro produced a body that was ultra-crisp with few angles in sight, yet not so way-out that it would date rapidly.

Leiding saw very little he wished to change. Giugiaro's rectangular headlamps were substituted for round ones, his expensive-to-produce bumpers were modified and the rear light clusters were reduced slightly in size. Key characteristics, such as the substantial C pillars and the steeply inclined rear to ensure the hatch was easily accessible, remained as Giugiaro had designed them. At the Golf's launch it was claimed that in the region of 100 prototypes had been built and that in excess of 4 million kilometres had been driven, either by these vehicles or especially adapted cars from other stables fitted with VW components.

Before and at the time of the launch it was essential that as many as possible aficionados of the Beetle, plus potential purchasers who appreciated VW's reputation but wouldn't have been seen dead in something so antiquated and uncomfortable, were informed about and tempted by what was behind Wolfsburg's fully functional portcullis. A brochure featuring both artists' impressions and cutaway diagrams of the Golf, not to mention what appears to be a studio-doctored sideways shot of a prototype on the cover and given the appropriate title of 'The little Golf ABC – A basic course in Golf', duly appeared. Those marketing gurus behind this publication cleverly enticed but didn't blind customers with overly technical detail. They also sewed a seed of potentially deliberate confusion by suggesting the car had been named after the game with use of the words 'basic course'.

'Das kleine Golf ABC. Ein Grundlehrgang in Golf, – The little Golf ABC. A basic course in Golf.'

The cover of one of the first brochures designed to market the Golf. The way the brochure's title is presented helped to perpetuate the theory that the car was named in honour of the game of golf, rather than after the Gulf Stream.

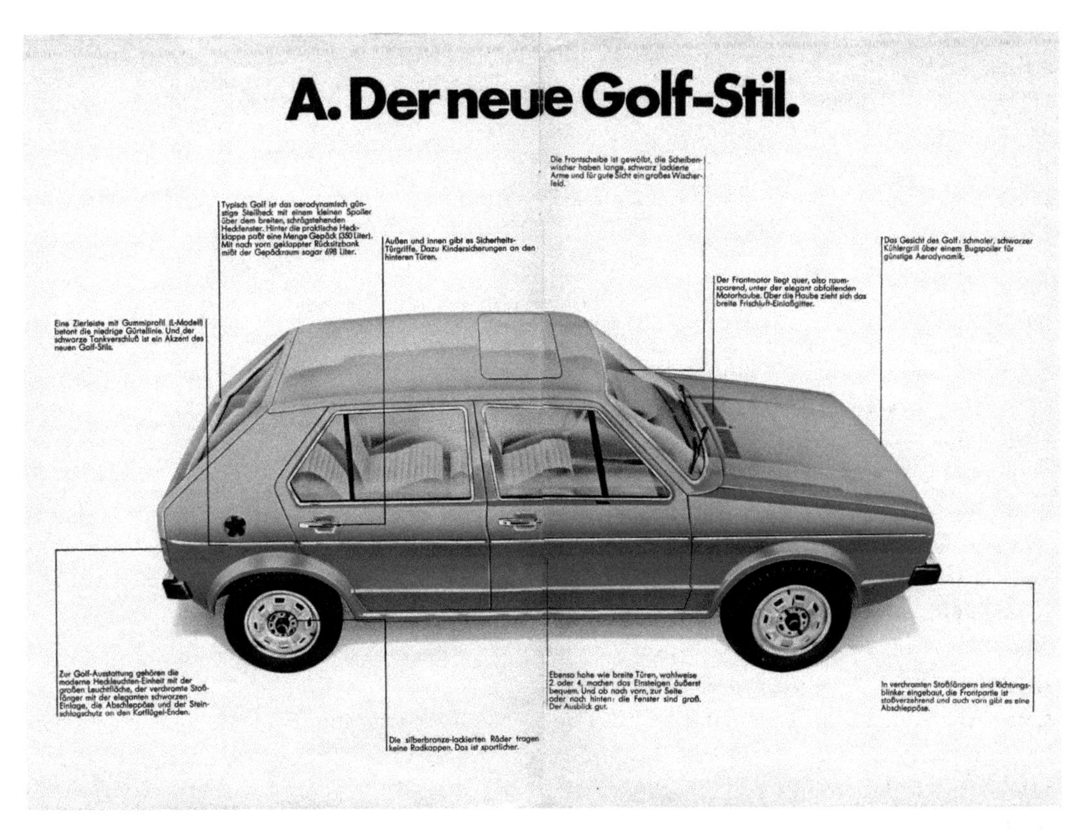

The exterior of the Golf was all about style. Modern rear lights, a hatch to access a spacious boot, and a lack of hubcaps, to quote three examples. The absence of hubcaps was nothing to do with cost – it was sportier, according to the copywriter.

A: The style of the new Golf

'A decorative strip with a rubber profile emphasises the low waistline. And the black fuel cap is an indicator of the new Golf's style.

The Golf's equipment includes a modern rear light unit with a large illuminated area, chrome-plated bumpers with elegant black inserts, a towing eye and stone-chip protection on the bumper ends.

The aerodynamically efficient hatchback with a small spoiler over the wide, sloping rear window is typical of the Golf. A lot of luggage (350 litres) fits behind the practical tailgate. With the rear seat folded forward, the luggage compartment measures 698 litres.

Outside and inside there are security door handles, plus child safety locks on the rear doors.

The silver-bronze painted wheels do not have hubcaps. That's sportier.

The windscreen wipers have long, black-painted arms and offer a large sweep for good visibility.

The doors – two or four – are as tall as they are wide, make getting in and out extremely easy. And whether to the front, to the side, or to the rear, the windows are large. Visibility is good all round.

The front engine is positioned transversely, i.e. to save space, under the elegantly sloping bonnet. The wide fresh air inlet grille extends over the bonnet.'The face of the Golf: narrow, black radiator grille over a front spoiler for favourable aerodynamics.

Direction indicators are installed in chrome-plated bumpers, the front end is shock-absorbing and there is also a towing eye in front.'

B: The new Golf's equipment

'Even the basic models of the new Golf offer equipment levels that are by no means always a matter of course in this class. The luxury "L" level of equipment includes, for example, quality carpets, a lockable and illuminated glove-box, seats that offer a relaxing ride and a folding luggage compartment cover.

The spacious interior has two metres of seating space (from the accelerator pedal to the rear seat backrest), 1.30 m of shoulder room width (front and rear) and one metre of leg room (with the front seats in the middle position) in the rear.

Anatomically correct, multi-adjustable single seats at the front and a comfortable seat at the back entice you to sit down. The seats are upholstered with non-slip corduroy - in the "L" version they have faux-leather side bolsters.

What to us today might be described as a spartan interior was lauded as particularly rich for cars in the Golf's class. Hardcore Beetle enthusiasts voted with their feet, but new markets were suitably impressed.

The steering wheel has an easy-grip cover ("L" model).

The convenient steering column switch for the windscreen wiper system has a two-stage switch and a single wipe contact as standard. An electric pump for the windshield wiper system is available as an extra.

For safety reasons, the steering wheel sits on a three-part steering column connected by universal joints.

The dashboard is deformable and padded with foam ("L" model). Clear instruments and indicator lights, plus easy-to-reach, impact-proof switches and levers make operation functional and safe.

With 8.0 or 8.5 litres of normal petrol (according to DIN), both engine versions are very economical in consumption. They are particularly economical at a constant speed of 80 km/h: 5.5 or 5.9 litres per 100 km.

The Golf is available with either a 50 PS or 70 PS ("S" model) engine.'

C: The new Golf – Technical Details

'The Golf draws its character from a sporty, lively yet robust and low-maintenance high-performance engine with amazing performance. The fastest version (1.5 litre/70 PS),

When it came to technical talk the message was essentially that the Golf was both faster and less thirsty than the Beetle. The space saving, space creating transverse nature of the engine wasn't overlooked, or the safety aspect of suitably powerful brakes.

the Golf ("S"), has a top speed of 160 km/h and goes from zero to 100 km/h in 12.8 seconds. Its wheels are individually suspended, the suspension harmoniously tuned; its track is wide, the wheelbase long, so the road holding is safe.

Also completely new is the torsion beam rear axle with easily replaceable axle body in T-profile and built-in stabiliser effect.

The powerful braking system of the "S" models has disc brakes at the front, a brake booster and, for safety's sake, two diagonally divided brake circuits.

A powerful generator supplies the electrical needs. The central electrical system is housed in a particularly clear and easily accessible manner.

The drive links to the front wheels directly, hence the excellent traction of the drive wheels. In addition, the front-wheel drive block balances the weight of the cargo held in the boot at the rear. That's why the Golf doesn't 'kneel' either in front or behind.

The Golf has a modern strut front axle with wishbones and negative scrub radius - hence the good directional stability and safe steering behaviour. And it has smooth rack and pinion steering - hence the exact curve guidance.'

Picking up more-or-less where the brochure left off, VW annexed a modified version of the 1,471cc four-cylinder engine from Audi and used it to power the top of the range Golf. *Autocar*'s road test reported a top speed of 98 mph and a 0–60 time of a very respectable 12.5 seconds. The smaller engine, which VW perceived to be the volume seller, was

A VW-produced advertising postcard once again linked the car to the game of Golf in a witty way.

The fastest Beetles developed 50 PS. Golf customers were directed to the more powerful 70 PS engine and its attendant higher trim level.

Above, above right and below right:
A selection of early Golf press shots – as the hatch was important, plenty of shots showed the rear of the car. There was also an emphasis placed on the car's versatility to accommodate both parcels and occupants. Note the car photographed is a three-door model, at the launch deemed likely to outsell its five-door sibling.

initiated at Audi for use in the 50 (think VW Polo) but honed at Wolfsburg. A SOHC engine, with a cast-iron block and alloy cylinder head, it displaced 1,093cc from a bore and stroke of 69.5 × 72 mm and had a compression ratio of 8.1. By coincidence, its maximum output of 50 PS was identical to that of the larger-engined Beetle, the 1600. However, its top speed of 91 mph and fuel economy of well over 30 mpg set it well apart from its ancestor.

Conventionality ruled the roost in terms of suspension with MacPherson struts, wishbones and coil springs at the front. At the rear, trailing arms with a transverse piece to link the two, plus integrated coil springs and shock absorbers, were the order of the day. Most decided that the rear suspension was notably stiff, this being a result of a deliberate attempt to minimise the understeer associated with all front-wheel-drive cars.

'The Golf. An attractive saloon and a practical estate... It lets you handle all but the biggest loads quickly and easily.'

'Golf trips are fast with an economical return.' The idea of fifteen or thirty small images being used to illustrate a single point spread to other members of the VW family, including the Beetle.

Perhaps unsurprisingly, the brochure text glided over the braking system as applied to the more basic model, for this featured drums all round. Fortunately, the more powerful option's system comprised servo-assisted discs upfront, but only offered drums at the rear.

It is also worth noting just how austere the interior of the base model was, while the brochure's claim that the 'L' specification was particularly rich failed to take into account the specification of cars produced in Japan which were noted for their gadgetry and magpie-attracting trinkets.

Please refer to the chart on page 32 with regard to dimensions and weights.

Onwards and upwards

If the Golf had minor failings when launched – and what car didn't and doesn't – the buying public at home and abroad were nevertheless sufficiently convinced that by October 1976 the millionth example was rolling off the assembly line. Overall Golf production numbers and sales figures are contained in the chart on page 30. Far from sleeping under new Volkswagen boss Schmücker's watchful eye, not only did the Golf receive a facelift in 1980, but also underwent a series of performance enhancing engine transplants. Extra models, ranging from the inspirational and niche market to the mundane and assumedly trendy, made the headlines.

With the Golf's 1980 facelift Volkswagen took a further giant and probably final step towards joining the rest of the automotive world in outlook. Nordhoff's Volkswagen had relied entirely on year-by-year technical improvements. To Nordhoff 'hysterical stylists'

'The Golf. There's more inside than meets the eye.' The picture depicts the most basic of Golf's, but to VW it featured 'trendy checkered seating, a high level of equipment, neat door pulls, a heated rear window, front and rear spoilers and reclining front seats.'

A post-1980 Golf could be distinguished by its moulded plastic wraparound bumpers. As a CL model the car also featured a silvery trim line on the bumpers, side impact strips and the hatch. Inside the CL enticed with such luxuries as a trip mileage recorder and lockable glove box.

signified built-in obsolescence. His disregard for the breed served Volkswagen well for the duration of his twenty years in charge, but such a policy was out of kilter with the policies of other manufacturers.

In 1980 out went the original bumpers, their replacements being of a wraparound nature, more elegant in appearance and contemporary in design with their plastic covers. Larger headlamps and wider taillight clusters may have had practical advantages; a restyled dash – albeit with additional gadgetry for more pricey models such as the GTi – could easily be regarded as superfluous. In the same category, so too could have been new seat and door trims.

October 1979 had seen the arrival of a 60 PS 1,272cc engine for higher spec manual cars, replacing the 70 PS 1,457cc, which, however, was retained for Golfs with an automatic box. With different markets in mind, the 1300 offered a drop in top speed from 97 to 93 mph and perhaps more significant, a tailing off in performance with 0–62 mph taking 13.5 seconds (compared to 12.7 for the 1500). Of course, power and acceleration was now the province of the GTi. Nevertheless, there was general criticism of the 1300 engine due to its lack of refinement.

1980 also saw the as yet unmentioned diesel-engined variant of the Golf receive an increase of 4 PS thanks to a leisurely leap from a 1.5 litre power unit to 1.6 litres. The diesel Golf was launched in September 1976 and, all credit to VW, went a good way to breaking the tradition of exceptional noise and sluggish behaviour more suited to tractors and their like. Nevertheless, what was produced was far from comparable with the models of later years. The diesel in 1.5 litre guise took a lengthy 18 seconds to crawl its way to 62 mph, but did offer a top speed of 87 mph when fully wound up. Of course, economy was the main reason to buy a diesel at the time, but thanks to the premiums involved in building the engine, plus various governments' Scrooge-like levy on diesel fuel, even *Autocar*'s claimed average of 46 mpg (compared to the 1100 petrol engine's 33 mpg) wasn't sufficient for many to turn in its direction.

1982 witnessed the arrival of a new breed of diesel – one capable of 96 mph and 0–62 mph in 13.5 seconds, but that still retained more than a modicum of fuel economy. Branded the GTD (in homage to the GTi and only available in LHD form), the initials, of course, revealed the addition of a turbo. Based on the existing 1.6 litre diesel engine, the TD required in the region of thirty changes to accommodate either a Garrett or KKK turbocharger. These included a more powerful oil pump, a larger oil circuit and cooler, plus the reinforcement of all areas affected by the higher exhaust gas temperature. A top speed of 96 mph and a 0–62 mph burnout of 13.5 seconds in all honesty was still leisurely. Dressing the car up with some of the GTi's hallmark looks – wider wheels, wheel-arch extensions and interior trim – was probably sufficient to hoodwink a few, if not that many. The real story was one of what was to come now the idea was lodged in various heads.

1979 saw the arrival of a Golf often described latterly as a model ahead of its time. This was the Formel E, a car that, as VW chose to put it, 'introduces economy with a capital E.' According to VW its 1100 engine 'compressed the air/petrol mixture to a higher degree than normal', extracting maximum energy from a minimum of fuel. This engine was connected to a new gearbox that featured three 'standard' forward gears and long-legged fourth for cruising. Associated gimmickry included a special front spoiler, aerodynamic pillar covers, a gear-change/fuel consumption indicator on the dash and, of course, a badge on the back proclaiming the purchaser's impeccable credentials. Needless to say, with performance equating to that of a wet fart, brochures made no reference to maximum speeds or 0–62 mph achievement.

Although the Mk 1 GTi hasn't been discussed yet, owners could also purchase the limited edition VW Driver, a GTi lookalike up to a point – think wheel arch trims, for example – but with a basic 1300 engine, rather than the GTi's fuel injection powerhouse.

An integral, but niche market, part of Volkswagen's range from the start had been a Cabriolet. Nordhoff, for many years unable to meet demand for the tin-top Beetle, had wisely listened to the eager overtures of two firms of coachbuilders, both desperate to contribute a soft-top version of the Volkswagen. He granted production of a four-seater Cabriolet to Wilhelm Karmann GmbH of Osnabrück and a soft-top coupé to Hebmüller. Sadly, the latter quickly fell by the wayside, but Karmann worked with Volkswagen throughout the Nordhoff years and by the time of the introduction of the Golf were still churning out soft-top Beetles, as well as assembling the Scirocco on VW's behalf.

Although popular in a bespoke sort of way, inevitably Beetle Cabriolet production couldn't go on indefinitely after the demise of the saloon, especially as the soft-top was based on the MacPherson strut, curved window, and plastic dash version of the car that had been axed in the summer of 1975. For Leiding a soft-top version of the Golf was not a top priority and nor was it for Schmücker. Nevertheless, during 1976 boffins behind the scenes at Wolfsburg and, of course, Karmann set about taking the top off the Golf. Much more of a challenge when compared to the Beetle with its separate chassis, there was considerable strengthening work to do to what remained of the shell, with some 90 kg worth of extra pressings. Additionally, and crucial if the Cabriolet was to be sold in the USA, was a rollover bar (welded both to the stiffening sills and strengthened sheet metal of the car), which ensured the Cabrio sailed through the strict rollover test for all varieties of car as decreed in the United States Federal Motor Vehicle Safety Standard 208.

The Mk 1 Cabriolet Golf was destined to outlive all other versions, only finally being replaced when the Mk 3 Golf made its debut. The face-lifted example pictured here dates from 1987, well into the production run of the Mk 2 tin-top Golf.

Launched at the Geneva Motor Show in March 1979, it could be requested – dependent on the market – with the 70 PS 1.5 litre engine, or more interestingly as a GLI (for which read a GTi without the hallmark trappings of the hot hatch). The 1100 engine was also available, but only in those markets where there was a tax advantage to be had by requesting an engine that might struggle with the Cabriolet's extra weight.

Due to the cost implications of producing a new model, the Mk 1 Cabriolet lived on through the years of the Mk 2 Golf, only finally being replaced by a soft-top based on the Mk 3 Golf, launched at the Frankfurt Motor Show in September 1993.

Two more models are worthy of mention. The first, a booted version of the Golf, is covered in Chapter Six when in Europe the car was called the Bora. The first booted Golf, launched in 1979, well within Mk 1 territory, was given the name Jetta, a name it retained throughout in what was to become its most significant market, the USA.

The other notable Golf Mk 1 was not a product of the Wolfsburg factory but instead arrived on the scene in 1978 via Volkswagen of South Africa and its Uitenhage factory. Concerned that the Mk 2 Golf would be bigger, heavier and cost more than the popular Mk 1, with Director General Carl Hahn's approval South Africa developed the Citi Golf, a Mk 1 available in one spec (a five-door, with 1300 engine) entry level kind of car. Such was the sales success of this model that a succession of Citi cars followed – even including a version of the GTi branded as the CTi. Amazingly, production continued until 2009, some twenty-six years after the end of German production and outliving all the generations of Golf covered in other chapters.

During the lifetime of the Mk 1 Golf the number of trim options and engines available had grown considerably, while specials such as the Golf Driver (an ordinary Golf in GTi clothing) and the Golf GX, (a 1500, five-door option with an economy gearbox and all the available executive-look bits of trim) helped generate further sales. Production eventually ended in October 1983, three months after a new car with the Golf name started to roll off the assembly line.

The tale of the Rabbit

If ever there was a missed sales opportunity for VW it came in the USA with the transition from air- to water-cooling. The 1973 oil crisis triggered the hitherto buoyant Bug's decline, as Toyota flooded the market with small cars both cheaper to buy and considerably more economical to fuel. A further nail in the coffin came when Gerald Ford took office as President in August 1974 and pressed domestic manufacturers to increase fuel efficiency by 40 per cent, or face condemnatory legislation. However, there were still more factors surrounding the Bug's exit. The US's growing addiction to emission controls would inevitably make it impossible to sell the air-cooled car at some stage and, of course, Wolfsburg had already decided that in Europe VW would be led by the Golf.

Until the oil crisis Bug year-on-year sales had risen steadily, 1966 being the first occasion when the figure topped 300,000 cars, before peaking in 1968 at 399,674. 1973 still saw a healthy 350,357 Bugs sold, but this was the final lull before the storm. The purchase and running cost related sales drop came in 1974 when 226,098 cars left the US showrooms.

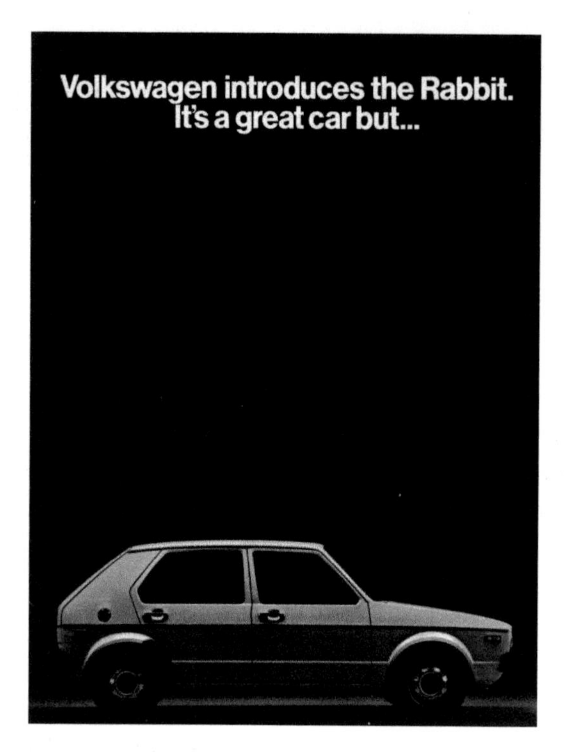

For reasons best known to Volkswagen, the Mk 1 Golf was known by the fluffy name of Rabbit in the USA. Easy to identify by its side repeaters and much heavier, girder like bumpers, brochure text was characteristically charismatic, but unfortunately did little to boost sales. This is the cover.

Rather than release the Golf – renamed for the US market as a cuddly bunny or Rabbit – at the same time as European market LHD cars, the Bug's replacement didn't debut until January 1975, obviously allowing Toyota and others to gain a stronger toehold. Likewise, it is fair to say that US drivers didn't share the love affair with a rear hatch that was starting to sweep through Europe. To Volkswagen's chagrin it was the last months of 1979 before a booted Rabbit, the Jetta, became available. A further negative in a land of powerful cars, in the USA the GTi didn't make its debut until the 1983 model.

Admittedly, there was little Volkswagen could do about the strength of the Deutsche Mark, which would inevitably depress US sales, but the fact that an extensive recall programme of 1975 Rabbits was necessary in 1976 could be laid at Wolfsburg's door. The issue related to engine-mount problems, while both carburettor and driveline modifications were required to cure stalling and starting issues. Confidence in the marque declined accordingly.

The ongoing issue of the Rabbit's purchase price dictated by its build location led Schmücker and Co. to revive Leiding's idea of turning to domestic US production. Schmücker purchased a brand new factory Chrysler had built but never occupied, naming it the Westmoreland assembly plant. Engines and transmissions were shipped in from Germany, but the rest was home-grown. The first US Rabbits rolled off the assembly line in 1978, hallmarked by less supportive, poorly made and generally cheaper seats, a colour-coded dashboard of poor manufacture, softer springing, and problems with valve guide seals (leading to engines which burnt oil, or worse still expired all together). All that was needed was premature rusting, which duly came, but wasn't necessarily confined to Rabbits built at Westmoreland.

'It may be hard getting used to a Volkswagen that can go 93 mph.'

Despite such disappointments Rabbit sales were reasonably buoyant, with 149,170 examples sold in 1978, rising to 214,835 the following year. However, by 1982 figures were tumbling, a mere 91,166 cars being sold – only the relatively recent Jetta holding its own. Carl Hahn, successor to Schmücker and already a big name from the air-cooled years, appreciated that the US market wanted a European specification when buying a car whether the vehicle was built at Westmoreland or Wolfsburg. Only the very late arrival of the GTi helped to boost sales. Even so, as the USA became aware of a new generation of Golf on the horizon, customers shied away from purchasing the outgoing model. In 1984 US sales tumbled to just 68,362, heralding an end to the name Rabbit and foretelling a very chequered sales history for VW throughout the decades. The Westmoreland plant with its history of significant losses, not to mention operating at well below capacity, finally closed its doors in 1987.

Rabbit Marketing © 1975 Volkswagen of America

While 1970s European markets were offered very much matter-of-fact, clinically clean sales brochures, the US continued to luxuriate in literature based on eye-catching headlines and witty text.

Here are a few tasters from one of the first Rabbit brochures.

Cover – 'Volkswagen introduces the Rabbit. It's a great car but...'

2/3 – 'It can get you into some tight spots.' (Text about the Rabbit's compact nature and the ease with which it can be parked)

4/5 – 'It may have more room than you care to have.' (Like room for the mother-in-law, her dog and an obnoxious bubblegum-blowing child)

6/7 – 'It may be hard getting used to a Volkswagen that can go 93 mph.' (Emphasising that here is a much faster and easy to drive car than the Bug)

'The guys at the gas station may forget your first name.'

8/9 – 'It may put your wife in the driver's seat.' (A theme no longer deemed appropriate – the little lady at home will also like the Rabbit)

10/11 – 'The guys at the gas station may forget your first name.' (The fuel economy of the Rabbit and more)

Four into one doesn't go

There can be no doubt that each generation of VW Golf has been a bestseller. There can be few other manufacturers who don't regard any car branded as a Golf as a challenging competitor to their own offerings. Volkswagen's published production numbers illustrate why. Sales figures were equally convincing.

VW's Published Golf Production Numbers					
1974 189,890	**1979** 833,625	**1984** 685,303	**1989** 890,158	**1994** 853,940	**1999** 841,625
1975 419,620	**1980** 831,527	**1985** 790,342	**1990** 896,874	**1995** 815,875	**2000** 915,383
1976 527,084	**1981** 799,287	**1986** 891,466	**1991** 808,100	**1996** 828,574	**2001** 855,368
1977 553,989	**1982** 656,359	**1987** 907,753	**1992** 927,286	**1997** 625,336	**2002** 774,718
1978 714,947	**1983** 626,797	**1988** 887,679	**1993** 795,616	**1998** 894,540	**2003** 774,718* Includes early Mk 5 models
Total number of cars produced under the Golf brand - generations one to four (plus early months of Mk 5 production in 2003) - 22,813,779					

Left to right – four, three, two and one – one car or four?

VW's Published Golf Sales Figures (all variants)				
	Mk 1 Golf 1974–1983	Mk 2 Golf 1983–1991	Mk 3 Golf 1991–1997	Mk 4 Golf 1997–2003
Sales figures in millions	**6.99**	**6.30**	**4.83**	**4.99**
	Note that the apparent decline in the Golf's popularity between models is explained by the number of years each generation was available – **Total Sales: 23.11 million**			

As is often the case, even taking into account rounding and calendar years, as opposed to sales periods, the figures don't quite tally. However, on 25 June 2002 Wolfsburg declared that the Golf had overtaken the legendary Beetle as the world's 'most often produced Volkswagen-model' with a grand total of 21,517,415 units having been built. 'Almost 40,000 employees in the plants in Wolfsburg, Mosel, Brussels, Bratislava, Uitenhage and Curitiba produce more than 3,600 Golfs every working day' was the boast.

It is an undisputed fact that Beetle production finally ground to a halt in its last stronghold, Mexico, on Wednesday 30 July 2003 at 9:05 a.m., when the final such car – number 21,529,464 – was presented to the world's press and anyone else who might have been interested.

Overlooking Wolfsburg's somewhat premature declaration of supremacy for the Golf, the relative snail pace of Beetle production, without hope of a sudden revival, confirming that an example of the fourth generation car would indeed overtake that grand total of the car christened Der Weltmeister, some still questioned the authenticity of Volkswagen's claim.

While a process of continual evolution had resulted in few if any parts of the Beetle produced in 1945 being still current in 2003, nevertheless an early example of the car was instantly recognisable as the same vehicle nearly sixty years later. The truth of the matter was that the first car to carry Golf branding was not the same vehicle as its successor and while each subsequent generation carried characteristics that helped to create a familiar family look, they were different cars that just happened to share a name. The chart below serves to illustrate a fact that to this day Volkswagen attempt to avoid, while questioning Toyota's claims regarding the many different bodyshells given the name Corolla as a contender to the title.

Technical specifications – Dimensions and Gross Weights							
	Mk 1 Launch	**Mk 1 Rabbit**	**Mk 1 Final year**	**Mk 1 GTi Final year**	**Mk 2 Launch**	**Mk 3 Launch**	**Mk 4 Launch**
Dimensions							
Length	3,708	3,945	3,815	3,815	3,985	4,020	4,149
Width	1,610	1,610	1,610	1,628	1,665	1,695	1,735
Height	1,410	1,410	1,410	1,394	1,415	1,425	1,439
Wheelbase	2,400	2,400	2,400	2,400	2,475	2,475	2,511
Track front	1,390	1,390	1,390	1,405	1,413	1,478	1,513
Track rear	1,350	1,350	1,358	1,372	1,408	1,462	1,494
Weight							
Gross	1,200 to 1,250 * According to trim levels		1,240	1,310	1,320	1,470	1,620 to 1,775 * E (basic) to V5 Auto
Dimensions in Millimetres and Weights in Kilos							

1976–1983: Mk 1 – 'The Golf GTi. Equipped for Competitive Sport'

The Golf GTI. Nine seconds to get to know it.

We were convinced that there must be a few smart men and women around who are looking for a thoroughly thoroughbred, elegant car. But one which does not require them to do without the solid advantages that owning a Volkswagen brings with it.

It was for these people that we developed the Golf GTI—a performance to crown the brilliance of our brilliant Golf series. With 110 mph to be exact.

The Golf GTI is easy to get to know. Nine ticks of the second hand on your watch pass as you are pressed back into the sportily comfortable seats and the speedometer needle rises from 0 to 60. Fifty it reaches in a bare 6.1 seconds.

These are figures which signify a maximum of active safety when overtaking. And they are also likely to make their mark at circuit races and rallyes in the near future. Since the engine concept has what it takes to make a flying start into motor racing.

But for all that the Golf GTI is no high-strung nervous steed, since we are well aware that you will be driving it under normal traffic conditions and not on a race track. It has nerves of steel that enable it to take the stress of normal motoring without a murmur. And to keep you just as happy, we have made its equipment not sportily Spartan but sportingly lavish.

2

Printed in August 1976, the cover of the GTi brochure was plain orange with the message Golf GTi highlighted in black. The inside pages told the story starting with: 'The Golf GTi. Nine seconds to get to know it.'

The Golf GTi – those famous initials being taken from the Italian 'grand turismo iniezione', or grand tour injection – was not a part of Leiding's blueprint for the transformation from air- to water-cooling. Instead the hot hatch, a car that would sell to the tune of 456,690 units between the launch in 1976 and its replacement in 1983, was initially the brainchild of Alfons Löwenburg, the development and test engineer who was also responsible for Wolfsburg's press fleet, and VW's PR director Anton Konrad. In March 1973, the former memoed a group of VW's senior managers connected with research, development and trials, outlining what he thought were the essential ingredients of a sporty Golf and its possible place in the forthcoming regime of water-cooled cars. Of their number, the most senior of all – the head of research and development, Ernst Fiala – was probably the most sceptical, suggesting the time was not right. This left Hermann Hablitzel, a passenger car technologist for VW and someone who knew a great deal about the ongoing development of the Golf in general, to set up an after-hours working group with meetings being held away from the work environment. This group attracted further interest in the form of Gunter Kühl from the press department, suspension expert Herbert Schuster, known for his fine tuning abilities, Jürgen Adler, whose specialist skills in chassis analysis and interior robustness led to additional reinforcements of the shell, and the respected engine builder Franz Hauk, whose EA827 design of 1,471 capacity had been developed for the Audi 80 and

'The Golf GTi. 110 horses and not much feed.' The main picture might have been of the dashboard, but the accompanying story was one of relative fuel economy. '

subsequently borrowed for the more powerful of the two Golf models launched in 1974. Gunter Kühl, another press office recruit, sourced motorsport events where the prototype when ready would be able to compete.

The group developed what they termed as the Sport Golf. Power came from a twin-choke Solex carburettor Audi engine, the 1,588cc GT that developed 100 PS. Lower and stiffer suspension, different shock-absorbers and minor adjustments to Giugiaro's body in the form of a hefty front spoiler – not to mention a little assistance from tuners Bilstein and Kamei – all helped to create the pocket rocket its progenitors were keen to advocate.

Test reports suggested that the Sport Golf indeed lived up to its name and Fiala was persuaded to see the car in action at the vast Ehra-Lessien test track during the spring of 1975. However, his initial scepticism was merely compounded. Fiala was concerned about the harshness of the suspension and even more so about the excessive noise from the intake system. Rumour has it that Fiala went so far as to declare the car undriveable. However, eager to have something new to show at the IAA show in Frankfurt, set to open on 11 September, and aware that more senior managers were increasingly conscious of the ad-hoc project's existence, Fiala decided to proceed cautiously by involving Herbert Schäfer, VW's chief stylist and Herbert Schuster, the recently arrived test manager, urging them to ensure the finished project was less of a road-racer and more of a comfortable car with great performance potential.

Conveniently, to suit the emission requirements of the American market, both the Audi 80 GT and the Passat were set to adopt fuel injection – at the time widely regarded the province of luxury class cars. With the Bosch K-Jetronic system added to the recipe, the car offered 110 PS at 6,100 rpm and more significantly, if that was possible, reduced intake noise considerably. On 28 May 1975 the project became official, approval being granted from on high.

Extensive testing took place, ranging from hammering the Sports Golf across the Sahara to the harshness of freezing conditions in the arctic north and high-speed thrashings on German autobahns. No major and few minor issues were found.

Two more individuals deserve a mention in the story of the GTi's creation. Horst-Dieter Schwittlinsky, whose job as a marketer was to carry out customer research, was the individual responsible for the change from the off-the-cuff name of Sports Golf to the often emulated GTi moniker. It has to be assumed that it was also Schwittlinsky who advocated adopting the Italian language rather than making use of the mother tongue initials of GTE, Einspritzung being German for injection and thus potentially confusing the hot Golf with the notably different Audi GTE.

The other person, the first female to join team GTi, was Gunhild Liljequist. Before joining Volkswagen she had both studied porcelain painting and worked as a fashioner of chocolate boxes, hardly the normal route to a career as an automotive designer. Working under Schäfer she was directly responsible for the GTi's distinctive tartan upholstery – highly fashionable at the time thanks to the London fashion scene purloining the traditional patterns denoting clan membership north of the border. It is likely that she was also responsible for the golf ball gear knob, adding fire to the fable that the Golf's name referred to the sport, and the distinctive three-spoke 'spittoon' design steering wheel. For his part Schäfer appears to have taken credit for the much-coveted red stripe around

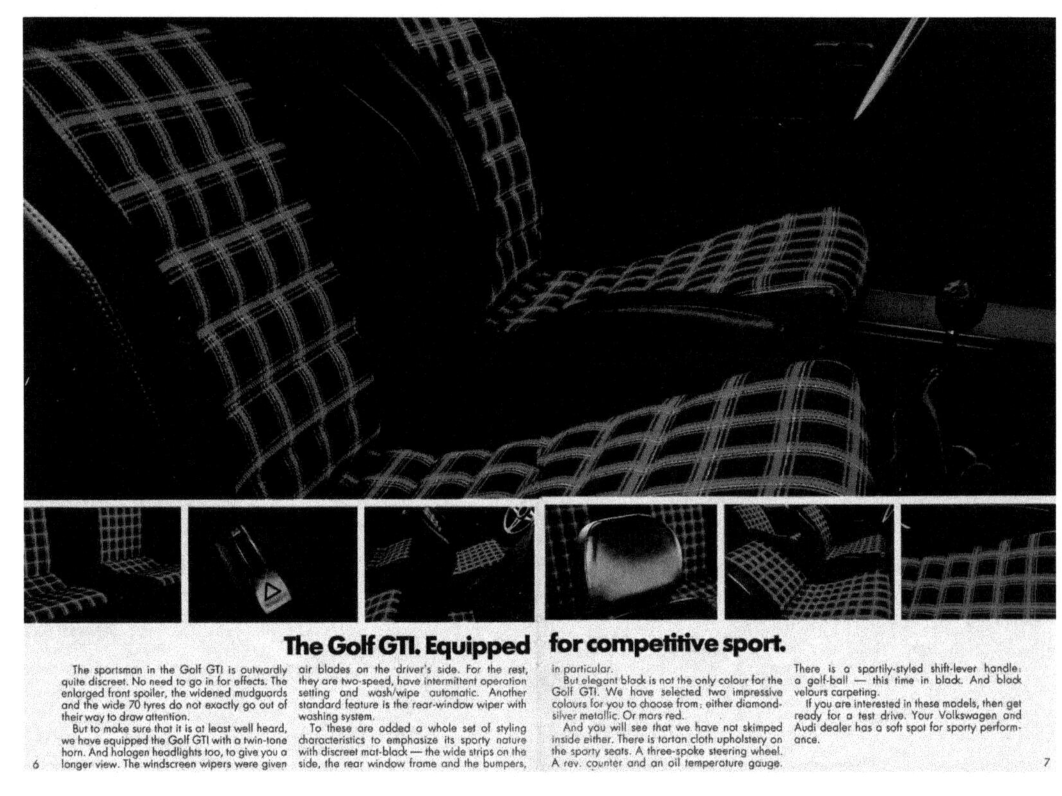

Sadly, the tartan upholstery didn't last that long either as part of the sporty concept for the GTi's interior, or with the natural wear and tear of being sat on!

the radiator grille, itself conveniently finished in black just like those of its siblings, and the black plastic wheel arch trims, plus a black stripe that ran between the wheel arches on the lower door panels. A black vinyl surround applied to the hatch window, plus the front spoiler being finished similarly in black, was sufficient to set the hot hatch apart externally. The decision to offer the GTi initially in just Mars Red and Diamond Silver served to highlight its individuality. The addition of black as a colour option a little later sadly detracted from the car's distinctive appearance, while months before the emergence of the second car to be named a GTi. British dealers could sell customers GTis in Alpine White, Helios Blue and Lhasa Green, as well as red, silver and black.

Exactly who completed the specification for the interior isn't certain. The standout feature was a sombre black headlining, which when coupled to a black dash, door panels, sun visors and, perhaps inevitably, carpet undoubtedly contrasted well with the loud if not garish tartan upholstery. Sports seats at the front fitted the bill perfectly. Sadly, the tartan upholstery didn't make it through to the end of the first GTi's production run.

While most distinguishing aspects of the GTi, either aesthetically or performance wise, are itemised above, it does no harm to summarise the latter, making it easier to compare the hot hatch with the rest of the range covered in this chapter. Comparisons to the abilities of later Golf GTis are also made easier, but hopefully it also serves to suggest that although small car performance-orientated versions of other marques existed, the Mini Cooper

Here's the Mk 1 GTi with bigger bumpers, a look that appeals more to current day tastes. Note the simple steel wheels – definitely unacceptable today.

being a prime example, and luxury sports cars at considerable price tags were available, Volkswagen's recipe offered a unique combination of usable power and the unprecedented distinction of fuel injection.

The summary performance Mk 1 GTi comparison chart includes details of a new larger 1800 engine for the GTi introduced in the dying months of 1982. Other changes made to the first GTi specification during its lifetime included the replacement of the four-speed box with five gears for 1980 models – a welcome move to keep engine revs down when cruising at law contravening speeds – only for the ratios to be revised again when mated to the additional torque generated by the 1.8 engine.

It should also be noted that the respected British magazine *Autocar* produced its own test figures, which varied from Volkswagen's at the time and still do when compared to the factory's telling of the GTi story today, usually to announce a new model.

The first Volkswagen Golf GTi	Specification at launch	Specification at the end of production	Comments
Capacity	1.6, 1,588cc [1]	1.8, 1,780cc [2]	[1] Mated to a close ratio four-speed gearbox until the 1980 model year, then five-speed from August 1979. [2] From 1982
Bore and Stroke	79.5 × 80 mm	81 × 86.4 mm	

The first Volkswagen Golf GTi	Specification at launch	Specification at the end of production	Comments
Compression Ratio	9.5: 1	10:1	
Max Output	110 PS @ 6,100 rpm	112 PS @ 5,800 rpm	
Maximum Torque	140 Nm @ 5,000 rpm	153 Nm @ 3,500 rpm °	° The much lower peak in torque transformed the GTI's mid-range punch
Performance - 0–62 mph Maximum speed	9.4 seconds* 115* mph	8.2 seconds 114 mph	* by 1980 VW claimed 8.8 seconds, * but a top speed of only 112 mph
			Suspension lowered by 20 mm (some official VW documents state 15 mm) 239 mm ventilated discs at the front, anti-roll bars at front and rear.
Wheels and Tyres	5½J × 13, 175/70 HR 13	6J × 14[3], 185/60 HR 14[3]	[3] These wheels – alloys – were part of the package bestowed on run-out special models. In Germany the cars were known as the GTi Pirelli, in the UK as the GTi Campaign.

Autocar test figures			
	1600 GTi – four-speed box	1600 GTi – five-speed box	1800 GTi
Max Speed (mph)	108	111	113
0–60 mph (seconds)	9.8	9.0	8.3

A Diamond Silver car shows off the red trim-line around the car's grille. Note the Pirelli alloys and twin headlamps indicative of the desirable Campaign model (British name) of 1983 vintage.

This example of the Campaign model illustrates that black paint acquaints to silver-coloured side stripes. The car is resident in the Stiftung AutoMuseum in Wolfsburg, which is well worth a visit.

Despite the highly favourable reaction generated by press and public alike at the IAA, Schmücker's Volkswagen had still opted for the cautious approach and, when production began in June 1976, the manufacture of no more than 5,000 vehicles had been sanctioned. In other words, nothing above the number required to supply the dealership network with a limited run and to homologate the GTi for Group One Production Touring Car motor sport. Such prudence proved groundless and although figures vary between sources, it seems feasible to propose that more than double such a number was required, with considerably higher demand to follow. For example, in 1981 the suggestion is that in excess of 72,000 GTis were sold.

As seems to be the case only too often, not only did the British market have to wait until 1977 to purchase a GTi, but even then it was by special order only and the car when it duly arrived was a left hooker. It would be July 1979 before RHD models were produced. As if this transgression wasn't serious enough, that onetime key export market and money

Left and below: This British market brochure published in July 1983 and, complete with a LHD car and Wolfsburg registration plate, itemised exactly what was special about the Campaign model. Green tinted glass and a steel sliding sunroof aren't instantly apparent.

AN EXTRA SPECIAL GOLF GTi

The cult-setting Volkswagen Golf GTi has won more acclaim from the motoring writers than perhaps any other car on the road today – "It is unique in its class as a sophisticated, tasteful and refined sports saloon " (What Car? February 1983). To celebrate its success in 1983 Volkswagen are introducing a special edition GTi model.

Of course, power is provided by the truly renowned 1800 cc fuel injected engine – "It is no exaggeration to state that it is all things to all men: superbly smooth, tractable and refined at all speeds, outstandingly quiet and sweet-running at all times, very potent and still well-mannered when maximum performance is demanded" (What Car? February 1983) – coupled to a five speed close ratio gearbox. Top speed is 114 mph and 0-60 mph is reached in just 8.2 seconds.

This special GTi is equipped with twin front lamps, incorporating head and foglamps, green tinted glass and a steel sliding sunshine roof.

It is easily distinguished by the Pirelli styled 6 J x 14 alloy sports wheels and low profile Pirelli tyres.

Inside, it has body-hugging sports seats, black headlining and carpeting and twin interior adjustable door mirrors.

Instrumentation includes a rev. counter, digital clock, leather trimmed sports steering wheel and a golf ball gear knob. A digital computer that operates at the press of a button gives the driver information on distance travelled, average mpg, average mph, journey time, oil temperature and outside temperature.

And to illustrate Volkswagen's confidence in its products this special model, like all Volkswagens, comes with 12 months/unlimited mileage, 6 year body protection and 3 year paintwork warranties.

There has never been a better time to buy a Volkswagen Golf GTi – visit your local V.A.G dealer today.

generator, the USA, lagged even further behind, condemned to wait until the 1983 model year before their Rabbit GTi became available.

With the advent of a new Golf and a new GTi on the horizon, VW trundled out the equivalent of a variously named run-out model. In Germany it was the Golf GTi Pirelli, while here in Britain it was marketed as the Campaign. Performance-wise there was nothing new, but in terms of spec these limited edition cars were worth getting your hands on. Distinctive alloys with Pirelli 'P's around the perimeters and a double headlight grille (head and fog) were accompanied by a list of top notch trimmings. While Germany sold their 10,500 allocation in just six months, Britain, which had to make do with an allocation of just 1,000 cars, caused chaos by titivating standard GTi's with Campaign goodies and offering them under the Campaign umbrella – even though some of the paint shades on offer had not been part of Wolfsburg's recipe.

Mexico had its own GTi known as the GT. It sported a 1.8 litre, 85 PS engine with a single carburettor, capable of 0–62 mph in 12.32 seconds.

1983–1991: Mk 2 – 'How to Make a Bestseller Still Better'

If the first incarnation of the Golf is regarded as a ground-breaking trendsetter, not only as transportation for a family, but also as the front runner for the title of hot hatch, a bestseller almost everywhere its wheels touched the tarmac, its successor was equally important for a number of reasons.

Volkswagen approached Giugiaro, among others, to pitch designs for consideration, but in the end they selected the conservative work of in-house designer Herbert Schäffer. A possible conclusion to be drawn from the decision is that one radical design – the original Golf – was sufficient, despite the important need to offer more space in both the rear passenger area and the boot, as rival manufacturers consistently improved their offer.

That Schäffer's design achieved what was asked of him – the Mk 2 Golf was unquestionably larger in the necessary areas than the Mk 1 – aided acceptance of a car that looked similar to its predecessor, in preference to a radical new concept. Admittedly some

Cover of the unusually flimsy sixteen-page brochure that launched the Mk 2 Golf. The theme 'better' attracted twenty-five instances of new being 'better' than previously.

were disappointed, especially where Schäffer had retained or mimicked aspects of the Mk 1 they were not ecstatic about. The C pillar was a prime example, but in general a degree of conservatism was acknowledged as the way forward.

Confirmation that the Mk 1 would be replaced had been declared as long ago as 1978, just four years into the car's production run. Schäffer's design emulated the work of Giugiaro while adding rounding, in keeping with latest trends, and stretching to accommodate the requests set. It retained the distinctively large C pillar and the rearward chopped-off, easy access hatchback stance – accidentally or intentionally setting the rule of gentle evolution, rather than the dramatic change, barely recognisable, approach advocated by some competitors. However, it should be made clear that the Mk 2 was not a face-lifted Mk 1, as the chart on page 32 serves to illustrate. The body was longer by 170 mm and wider by 55 mm, the front track was similarly 23 mm wider and the rear was 50 mm wider. The wheelbase was 75 mm longer and the platform was different.

Notable changes for the better included a drop in drag coefficient from 0.42 to 0.34, the result of many trips to the wind tunnel, the already mentioned 'rounding', a smaller frontal area, and flush window glass. The rearward tidying offered an even steeper elevation of the hatch and consequently added to the boot's height, while the larger wheelbase facilitated more room for rear seat passengers or, with the backrests down, a further contribution to boot space that it was claimed equated to 30 per cent.

Claims that the new car was possessed of multiple new engines stretched the truth somewhat – a fairer declaration would have been to say those carried over were the subject of revision, heavy or otherwise, the performance of the GTi being a prime example. All that was announced in a typical Mk 2 launch brochure was that the 'top speed has been increased by 5 mph to 119 mph'. This can be considered a significant understatement. Omitted were references to the engine's greater flexibility, its always welcome boost in maximum power being delivered at lower rpm, and its valuable increase in torque kicking in at a lower engine speed. Drifting slightly from the specifics of the 1800 engine, spacing between fifth and the lower gear ratios was increased.

GTi 1800 Engines as specified late Mk 1 and new Mk2		
	Mk 1	Mk 2
Capacity	1780cc	1781cc
Bore and Stroke	81 × 86.4 mm	81 × 86.4 mm
Compression Ratio	10.0 : 1	10.0 : 1
Output	112 PS at 5,800 rpm	112 PS at 5,500 rpm
Maximum Torque	148 Nm at 3,500 rpm	155 Nm at 3,100 rpm
Top Speed	114 mph	119 mph
0-60 mph	8.2 seconds	8.3 seconds

At the other end of the scale to the GTi, the latest incarnation of the Formel E still smothered those with an interest in greenery, while the interesting 70 PS Turbo Diesel failed to make it to British shores again. Fortunately, a turbo-charged version of the 1.6 diesel engine was on the cards for 1985, an engine that would offer 70 PS, a top speed of

99 mph and could accomplish the 0–60 sprint in 13.5 seconds, all of which was at least a move in the right direction for the oil burning community.

Another early day's advance, at least as far as the British market was concerned, was the 1985 introduction of a more powerful GL spec car. Some even went as far as to say that here was a GTi for the respectable, for which read middle-aged man. Gone from the option list was the 1.6 GL and in its place paced a 1.8, a car with a top speed of 111 mph and capable of the 0–62 gallop in 9.8 seconds (compared to the previous 1600's figures of 104 mph and 12.0 seconds respectively). Maximum output leapt from 75 PS to 90 PS and, perhaps even more significantly, optimum torque was up from 125 Nm at 2,500 rpm to 145 Nm at 3,300 rpm. Of course, here was the GTi engine but without the oomph of fuel injection; a single carburettor, as per the rest of the range, was deemed sufficient.

Two further developments have to be mentioned, though neither is connected to performance or visual appearance. Following a heart attack in 1981 Schmücker had resigned. His successor Carl Hahn took over officially on 1 January 1982. Hahn, who joined Volkswagen from the tyre manufacturer Continental, had previously been a Nordhoff protégé and had made a big name for himself in the USA where he had been in charge for a number of years. To Hahn, naming the new Golf as the Rabbit again in North America didn't make commercial sense. As a brand, the Golf had been highly successful from day one and it was recognised as such the world over. The name Golf, whether mistaken as a game or correctly identified as a wind, suited the car. The cute and cuddly bunny inferences did not. The Rabbit brand's association with rust, unreliability and any other ill that could be thrown at it demanded as much distancing as possible. Hahn's word was final – the new car would carry the name Golf in the USA too.

In the same vein, Hahn was well aware of the USA's love for cars with 'trunks' – the traditional three-box shape – a fact in VW terms illustrated by the comparative success of the late arrival Mk 1 Jetta there. The decree came from Wolfsburg's thirteenth floor that the second-generation Jetta would debut as close as possible to the Golf's arrival. Having been designed alongside the new Golf, this wasn't a particular problem and the new Jetta made its first appearance in February 1984.

Before signing off the new Mk 2 Golf as a universally agreed improvement on its predecessor, it is worth noting that sections of the motoring press were initially less than enamoured by the new car. Chief among the criticisms levied at the Mk 2 was its appearance, with both the similarities between old and new and the general effects of an increase in weight being unfavourably judged. The even heftier C pillars, certainly not an essential aspect of the design engineered to keep the car structurally sound and frankly rather more of a stylist's whim, together with the reduction in the reduced size of the rear hatch glass, headed the more specific groans and gripes list. Writing with reference to the American spec car, the magazine *Road & Track* summed up the 'professional' mood well. 'The Golf', they said, 'doesn't look exciting. It doesn't look different.' Motor's summary added a further ingredient: 'the rounded lines lack the visual punch of the original. The car looks less handy, less fun.' Specific to the GTi, the AA's *Drive* magazine announced that it was epitomised by talk of its 'grey hairs'. 'It lack[ed] the seductive curving lines of its rivals' and 'would do absolutely nothing for your ego when standing at the kerb.' More of a similar nature could easily be dredged up from the archives, but the picture is clear.

However, as far as the buying public went, they were happy that the new Golf was easily recognisable as being from the same mould as its predecessor. The Mk 2 accordingly topped the production number tables and popularity charts. If there was a little behind the back murmuring from buyers rather than the automotive hacks, no doubt to the surprise of today's enthusiasts, this was largely reserved for, of all models, the GTi.

Volkswagen was increasingly in the business of offering more variations in terms of trim and performance to some markets, but not others. Inevitably, with Wolfsburg on its doorstep and devotion apparent for a home-bred product, German dealers demanded every engine and trim level available. Britain, as a RHD maverick, tended to receive models later than most, while the range was more restricted. Conversely, on occasion the UK spec for a given model may differ, even gaining items over and above that of the home market specification. Take it as read that not every variation of trim is covered for the Mk 1 Golf in Chapter Two. From Mk 2 days onwards, with variations and specials springing up like wildfire, please take it for granted that the text refers to the UK market ... unless, of course, a stunning Golf, available in LHD form only, just can't be omitted.

The chart on page 46 outlines the Golf Mk 2 offer for the British market as it stood at the launch date. As usual, as poor RHD relations, whereas Mk 2 cars were to be seen on German roads from 10 September 1983 – production having started in June – deliveries in Britain weren't due until March 1984. Curiously, the GTi didn't go into production for anyone until January 1984.

Spot the differences from basic to Sunday best. It's fairly hard going; the top-of-the-range GL does have tiny chromed hubcaps though.

Golf Mk 2 three- and five-door Hatchback Range at Launch (British market)				
Golf Standard [1]	3 door	1.05 litre	45 PS	4 speed [2]
C	3 door	1.3 litre	55 PS	4 speed [3]
C Formel E	5 door	1.3 litre	55 PS	4 speed
C Diesel	5 door	1.6 litre	54 PS	4 + E
CL	5 door	1.3 litre	55 PS	4 speed
GL	5 door	1.6 litre	75 PS	4 + E
GL Auto	5 door	1.6 litre	75 PS	Automatic
GTI	3 door	1.8 litre	112 PS	5 speed [2/3]
[1] Dropped in the summer of 1984. VW produced this option for markets where there was a tax advantage in running a car with a small engine.		[2/3] The GTI cost 71 per cent more than the Standard model and 58 per cent more than the 3 door 1300 with C level trim.		[1] VW in Britain added the Standard to herald the bargain price a new Golf could be purchased for. A more realistic comparison is to say that the GTi cost 58 per cent more than the C-spec

'The new Golf'

Without a great deal of angst, Volkswagen could write about and illustrate a total of twenty-five reasons why the Mk 2 Golf was even better than its predecessor – a feat that may be said to justify the title of their launch brochure as pictured on page 42. Each story contained within the brochure's sixteen pages was prefaced by the word better. Without reproducing the entire text, there follows the majority of the highlights (with, where necessary, explanatory notes in brackets).

Three new engines; 'Top speed is up'; Economy (greater, inevitably); Lower interior noise level; Controls and instruments (improved layout and additional equipment dependent on the model); Reduced maintenance; Heating and Ventilation (improved); 'Sheer space. The new Golf is bigger. It is longer and wider. The larger exterior has particularly benefitted the interior passenger area. There is more legroom, headroom and shoulder room. And doors are bigger for easier entry and exit'; Driving safety; Road-holding; 'The new Golf clings to the road even better than before with its longer wheelbase, wider front/rear track and further improved front and rear axle; Quieter – average engine speeds are lower; Luggage space (increased by 30 per cent); Fuel capacity (new plastic 12 gallon tank); Aerodynamics – 'With a Cd value of only 0.34, the new Golf leads its class'; 'The modified front axle layout

'Take a good look at the 1988 Golf ... You can see that there is a newly designed grille with wider slats and a larger Volkswagen logo ... A new design for the side rubbing strips enhances still further the stylish body-shape, as well as providing more effective protection for today's motoring. The quarter lights have been removed and the door mirrors repositioned...'

This early example of the top of the range GL (if you exclude the GTi) came with a new 1600 engine (that developed 75 PS) model. Hidden among the specification details was the news that with the arrival of the Mk 2, the GL model could be specified with central locking, power steering and electric windows – at extra cost, of course.

and wider track increase suspension travel for high standards of ride comfort.'; Corrosion protection; 'For instance, hot wax flooding of lower body cavities, plastic front wheel arch linings and effective undersealing...'; 'The redesigned rear light clusters enable a wider tailgate opening for easier loading...'; 'Rain channels – They are plastic and integrated into the roof of the new Golf to aid good aerodynamics'.

Above left: As a way of boosting already healthy sales, Volkswagen introduced various special models. One of the most impractical, but also trend-setting, was the Golf Match. The basic 1300 model gained various goodies associated with the GL as well as 'smartly tailored' white upholstery. Externally both the bumpers and door mirrors were colour-coded with the bodywork (almost a first), as were the wheels.

Above right: With the MK 3 Golf on the horizon up popped the Golf Ryder. 'Take a Golf 1300 ... Add the extras', shouted the copywriters. Those extras were Ryder name badges front and rear, steel sliding sunroof, split rear seat, twin headlights, special wheel trims, and special black diagonal velour upholstery.

One over par GTI

Returning to the GTi, the promise that a 16-valve version offering 130 PS was 'to follow' was intriguing but hardly sufficient to stop grumbles not necessarily about the late launch, but most certainly concerning the specification. Frankly, the new GTi's goody-bag list wasn't comparable. Gone were the twin headlamps of the run-out specials, dismissed were alloy wheels and bordering on dull was the upholstery – truth be told, visually it wasn't that different to the turbo-charged diesel Golf. Peeved punters voted with their feet and sales between Mk 1 and Mk 2 models tumbled by 30 per cent. Hahn acted quickly. Within a year of the Mk 2 GTi's launch the car had received a makeover – a facelift reinstating the status of GTi ownership – as well as a meeting with the can-opener, as a five-door version was added to the line-up.

An eight-page brochure of 1985 vintage reminded would-be owners of a GTi of its hot credentials. However, in answer to earlier criticism of the car not standing out from the crowd, a deluge (for VW at least) of new equipment was announced. This consisted of twin exhaust pipes, red trim-strips for the bumpers, wide side mouldings, black door sills and alloys (standard on the new five door GTi and at extra cost on the traditional three door offering). Inside, the latest style of upholstery was appropriate to the mood of the times.

Here is the UK sales pitch for the upgraded Mk 2, complete with difficult to word wheel details. Pirelli-styled alloys had been standard here in Britain unlike other markets and now they weren't for the equivalent model. Whoops!

> The GTi ... is immediately recognised by its red trimmed, twin headlamps grille ... New for 1985 is the addition of twin exhaust pipes, red trim stripes for the bumpers, a wide side moulding, steel sliding sunroof and sporty striped upholstery. An attractive 6J × 14 steel wheel is now offered as standard on the three door model with the option of specifying Pirelli styled alloy wheels. The alloy wheels are standard on the five door model.

More still was added to 1986 models, with a sliding sunroof becoming standard, as well as a larger front spoiler. Tinkering with the specification to keep mutinous troops at bay was all very well but what was really needed – in the light of the opposition striving hard to overtake the GTi – was more power. Enter the 16-valve GTi.

Work on the 16-valve engine project for the GTi had started as long ago as 1981. The technology wasn't new – Grand Prix Peugeots had been so endowed in 1912 – but most manufacturers thought 16 valves prohibitively expensive for a road car. However, if turbo charging – the way of most others – had been dismissed by VW for petrol engines on the basis of a combination of inadequate torque and heavy fuel consumption, a 16-valve engine

Above left: 'Volkswagen's swift Golf GTi has entered a new era, thanks to the development of a sophisticated new 16-valve engine ... the most powerful in its class.'

Above right: 'The Golf GTi has hip-hugging front sports seats designed for grand touring comfort.' The rather gloomy looking interior was, in reality, trimmed with a combination of black and red upholstery.

'The new power plant has been given four valves per cylinder to improve the gas flow by an estimated 20 per cent and thus increase tractability and power. The valves are operated by double overhead camshafts, as used in advanced racing engines...'

The arrival of the 16-valve GTi didn't scupper the prospects of the existing Mk 2 GTi (as pictured here). If the car had been a four-door model the alloys would have been standard equipment, but on a three-door model they were an extra-cost option.

The running gear of a LHD Golf GTi: the transverse engine layout led to extra room for passengers.

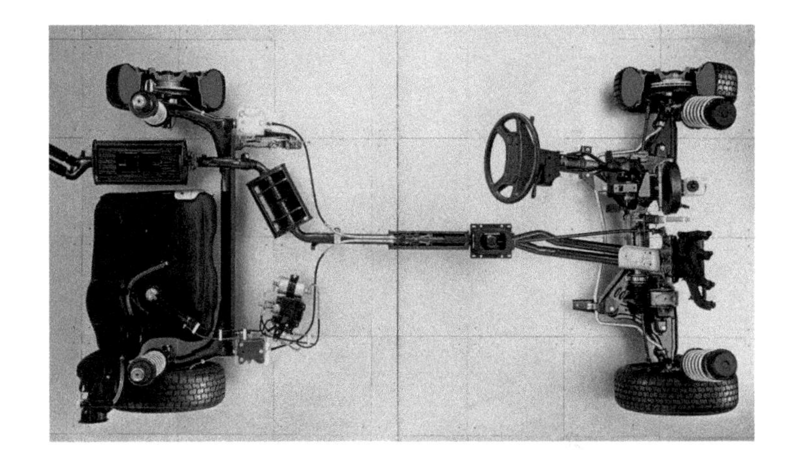

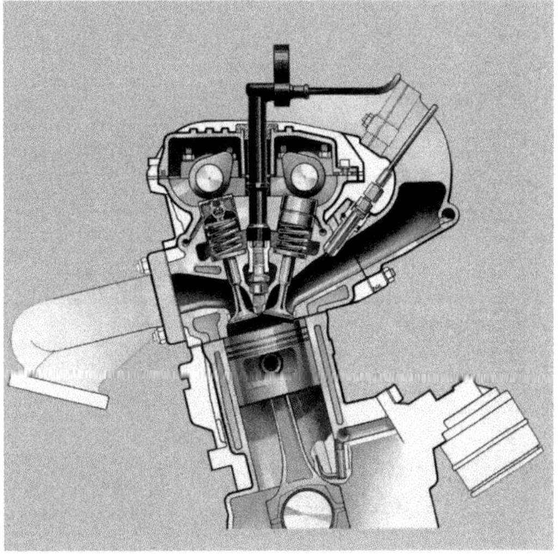

The GTi's engine in 16-valve guise – four valves per cylinder – offered low-down torque and the ability to perform effortlessly up to 7,200 rpm.

Towards the end of production of the Mk 2 and at a point when even the 16-valve GTi appeared eclipsed by more powerful models, only subtle points distinguished it from the rest of the pack. These were: the staple diet 16-valve badges front and rear; a roof-mounted aerial; BBS alloy wheels; and half-darkened rear light classes.

An example of the GTi produced for the American market. Note the rectangular headlamps and the side repeaters. Once appointed, the latest VW boss, Carl Hahn, instructed that the name Rabbit should no longer be used, as the image it portrayed was inappropriate.

Interior of the US market Volkswagen GTi *c.* 1985 – American salesmen tended to drop use of the word Golf when referring to the GTi. Options at extra cost included air-conditioning, power steering and cruise control.

was the logical way forward. The cylinder block was the same as that of the standard eight-valve engine, the difference came with the multi-valve head – two intake and two exhaust valves per cylinder – driven by twin-overhead camshafts. A larger oil pump, sodium-filled exhaust valves and oil jets playing on the underside of the piston crowns, while employing the same Bosch KA-Jetronic injection more or less tells the story.

A typical response to the 16-valve GTi's abilities having driven it was that of the magazine *Motor*. 'So long as the full range is used (the red line is set at a heady 7,200 rpm) the Golf's acceleration is stunning ... For the hard driving enthusiast, the extra top-end power does give the GTi that extra sparkle that's needed to take on the rapidly improving competition. It is capable, seamless, mature: strong on all-round ability and long term desirability. All told, it's still the best.'

The chart below illustrates why the addition of eight valves to the GTi was so worthwhile, even if there was a premium to pay for the honour.

Golf GTi 8-Valve v Golf GTi 16-Valve		
	8-Valve	**16-Valve**
Capacity	1.8, 1,781cc	1.8, 1,781cc
Bore/Stroke mm	81 × 86.4	81 × 86.4
Output PS at rpm	112 at 5,500	139 at 6,100
Compression	10.0:1	10.0:1
Max. Torque Nm at rpm	157 at 3,100	168 at 4,600
Valve gear	Single overhead camshaft, with maintenance-free hydraulic tappets.	Twin overhead Camshaft with two inlet and two exhaust valves per cylinder.
Induction	Mechanical fuel injection	Mechanical fuel injection
Transmission	five-speed close ratio, sports	five-speed close ratio, sports
Brakes	Diagonally divided dual circuit system with internally ventilated front disc brakes and rear disc brakes. Brake servo.	
Wheels/Tyres	6J × 14 – 185/60 HR 14	6J × 14 – 185/60 VR 14
Top speed mph 0–60 mph	119 8.3	129 7.9

Mk 2 facelift and loose ends

Assuming that few readers will have a particular interest in what Volkswagen did to keep the green environment lobby at bay, or for that matter how they accommodated drivers who had listened to people in high places who promoted the line that diesels were more environmentally friendly because they used less fuel than petrol cars, a brief mention of minor cosmetics in 1987 and again in 1989, plus a diversion into the infancy of a revolutionary four-wheel-drive system should suffice, before returning to the hot models.

The 1987 changes for the 1988 model year consisted of a redesigned grille with slats set further apart, a larger VW logo at both front and back, restyled side rubbing strips to 'enhance still further the stylish body-shape' (really), and quarter-lights removed (to give larger opening windows at the front). Inside, there was both a new steering wheel and steering control. The 1989 modifications centred on bulkier bumpers for the 'posh' GL spec cars and for the GTis. A stylist's dream and an engineer's complete waste of time, the purpose behind the change was to align selected Golf models with the corporate look already imposed on other cars in VW's range.

Following the arrival of the widely acclaimed Audi Quattro in 1980, schemes were developed to engineer a Golf offering both powerfully throaty vavoom and claw-like road grip. First though, as the Passat shared many of its characteristics with the Audi, that was an easier option. Pushing the Golf further down the ladder, the next pea out of the pod in 1985 was a Transporter with four-wheel drive, but obviously without racetrack attributes. However, whereas previously all-wheel drive had been designed to be permanent, for the Bus, the system developed in partnership between Volkswagen and the Austrian company Steyr Puch only brought the rear wheels into play when the going got tough. Invested with the name syncro – the small 's' is deliberate – the system centred around a viscous coupling, essentially a unit with two sets of plates that locked together linking the second set to the drive just as the first was and thus activating the rear wheels.

The Golf syncro, following in the Transporter's adhesive but not speedy footsteps, was launched at the Frankfurt show in September 1985. VW heralded the syncro as a four-wheel-drive system with 'slip sensitive power distribution'. Thanks to the hefty premium to be paid for the Golf syncro, making the car more expensive than a GTi, sales proved sluggish. Nevertheless, the syncro is worthy of mention, both for the part its technology played in the even hotter Mk 2 Golf story and as a concept of increasing significance in the development of the third car to carry the Golf moniker.

Hotter than hot Mk 2 Golfs

As a new decade began to glimmer on the far distant horizon, the pressure was on Volkswagen to keep pace with others in the demand for exceedingly fast, performance-driven hatchbacks. Hahn had been persuaded, if such a tactic was necessary, that success in motorsports would shower the company with an ever-increasing volume of sales.

Simplifying the story by excluding performance Polos', Passats', et al, a decision was taken to endow a hot Golf with a supercharger rather than a turbocharger, on the basis that the former offered boost at lower speeds and developed torque both earlier and later across the range. Volkswagen named their supercharger the G-Lader (Lader being the German word for a 'supercharger', an apparatus for increasing the volume of air over and above that normally drawn into the engine and G after the G-shaped spirals within the body of the supercharger unit). To this they appended the number 60 to indicate the height of the said spiral walls.

In order to compete in World Championship rallies, VW were obliged to present a minimum of 5,000 road-going examples of any souped-up car they created. Having initially spoken of a Super Golf back in 1988, the car that hit the dealerships – including an alleged 80 for the British market, but, of course, left hookers – were known as the Rallye Golf. The specification on page 57 reveals that while the car was unquestionably the most powerful

VW Golf built to date, the use of the syncro system and its attendant weight issues suggested a car hardly more powerful than the GTi. However, as delving into the figures demonstrates, a beneficial significant increase in torque existed, while four-wheel drive ensured the Rallye Golf clung to whatever surface was thrown at it.

The Rallye Golf was easy to distinguish from its siblings as it came with US-style rectangular headlamps, larger-than-life fully colour-coded bumpers, a particularly large front spoiler that

The cover of the Rallye Golf brochure published in English in 1990 – as only 5,000 LHD cars were produced, the car was a rarity then and is definitely so now.

To assume that the Golf Rallye was possessed of a substantial moulded body kit would be wrong: all the panels were made of metal.

'The performing art.' 'Based on the fabulously successful 1.8 litre four-cylinder Golf GTi engine, in its 1,763 cc supercharged version ... it has a power output of 160 bhp [PS].'

'Two aspects of the Rallye Golf lift it head and shoulders above the crowd – the G-charger and the syncro four wheel drive system. One creates the performance; the other allows the driver to use it!' Pictured is the G60 supercharger.

included built-in fog lamps, wider sill panels, a unique design of radiator grille, and, most expensively, all-metal wheel arch extension panels both front and rear.

In September 1989 what was essentially a front-wheel-drive-only Rallye Golf, without the extra external trimmings and more of a lookalike to the GTi twins, made its debut at the Frankfurt Motor Show. This was the GTi G60, not to be confused by a so limited edition G60 that at just seventy-five units and an enormous price tag, it deserves to be overlooked. Beneath the skin the GTi G60 varied in detail from both the Rallye Golf and the GTi as the chart serves to demonstrate. Cars making their way to British shores did so at the whim of a would-be individual owner and not courtesy of VW.

Rallye Golf and GTi G60 Specification		
	Rallye Golf	GTi G60
Capacity	1.8, 1,763cc	1.8, 1,781cc
Bore/stroke, mm	80.6 × 86.4	81.0 × 86.4
Max output	160 PS at 5,600 rpm	160 PS at 5,800 rpm
Max torque	225 Nm at 4,000 rpm	225 Nm at 3,800 rpm
Compression ratio	8.0:1	8.0
Induction	Digifant electronic fuel injection, G -charger, charge air cooling	Digifant electronic fuel injection, G -charger, charge air cooling
Top speed	130 mph	132 mph
Acceleration 0–62	7.6 seconds	8.6 seconds
Track mm	Front 1,429 Rear 1,434	Front 1,433 Rear 1,428
Wheels and Tyres	6J × 15, 205/50 15 VR	6J × 15, 185/55 R 15 V
Drive	Drive to front wheels via differential and half shafts with constant velocity joints. Drive to rear wheels via bevel gears, three piece propeller shaft and viscous coupling. Final drive with freewheel integrated between bevel gears and differential. Half shafts with constant velocity joints. Free-wheel lockup for four-wheel drive when reversing.	
Gross vehicle weight	1,640 kg	1,530 kg

Over the course of the last two years of Hahn's tenure as Director General – he retired at the end of 1992 aged sixty-six – a number of factors caused VW to think again about ever-more powerful and torque-laden offerings. The Rallye Golf had proved to be something of a damp squib on the race track, the 16-valve GTi mopped up the majority of GTi sales at the expense of the G60. Thanks to Hahn's rightful development of VW as a global force – he entered into a partnership with Škoda in 1991 – by 1993 profits hadn't just continued the tumble of 1992 but were gone, an unhealthy loss taking their place. Besides the thought process behind the next Golf, now not far away, would take the car in a totally different direction.

This well-known press publicity shot confirms how difficult it was to distinguish visually between the Golf GTi G60 (seen here) and the Golf GTi 16-valve. Behind the wheel it was a different matter.

The GTi G60 was only available in LHD form, but more than one version existed. Initially syncro was excluded from the specification, a risky business considering that the supercharger was pummelling 160 PS of naked power through the front wheels only.

Above left: The interior of the GTi G60 offers no clue to the potency of the car.

Above right: As the cover of this brochure dedicated to four-wheel-drive Golfs illustrates, the cars looked like any others. The syncro was not a hot hatch as its allocated engine, the 1,781cc 0–62 mph time of 10.3 seconds, confirms. Nor was the syncro-laden with spoilers and other sporty trimmings; it was simply a vehicle unaffected by adverse road conditions.

The viscous coupling 'consists of a drum-shaped housing, which is bolted to the prop shaft and contains fifty-nine steel plates with a force locking connection created by silicone oil. It is this which compensates for the small differences in speed between front and rear wheels ... that occur when cornering. Greater speed differences, when front wheels slip on a wet or icy road ... makes the connection between the plates even more rigid, automatically transferring the correct amount of drive to the rear axle...'

1991–1997: Mk 3 – 'Introducing a New Concept'

Most long-term VW enthusiasts will have been brought up on a diet laden with criticism of the third incarnation of the Golf, a car which was launched in August 1991 for the '92 model year. Britain first saw the new Golf in February 1992, while, thanks to production being transferred to Mexico for US cars, the Mk 3 debuted in America in the spring of 1994.

Autocar and *Motor* took at least three pops at Wolfsburg's finest in the early months of its production run, each creating ominous grey clouds that tended to lodge in the mind. In August 1991 the magazine declared that the car would demand 'getting used to a look that even the most devoted Golf fan would have to call "chunky".' The following month they described what they termed as the more affordable Golfs in the range as having 'lethargic' performance and 'compromised' handling. The cars lacked 'verve and sporting character', the steering was 'stodgy', there was 'more body roll than you'd expect'. The list seemed endlessly depressing. An encore in February 1992 offered a repeat of what had been said before, but this time stirred in a feeling about the Mk 3 no one – and there were plenty – as yet had been able to put into print. 'In a sense', the magazine proclaimed, 'the fun has gone out of it.'

Were such sentiments justified? Like its predecessor, the Mk 3 Golf was designed in-house and by the same lead man, Herbert Schäfer. His words on the subject have been recorded for

The flagship VR6 hardly stood out from the crowd externally. BBS alloys had found a home on the Mk 2 16-valve Golf GTi. Colour-coded items, such as the mirror housings and the radiator grille, were shared with new Mk 3 GTi.

posterity. 'As we moved from the first to the second Golf, we made the car bigger, installed more powerful engines and gave it better handling. In the third generation, design now plays a greater role. We found a look that is typical of the Golf, which radiates safety and quality.'

Read between the lines and it becomes clear that Volkswagen's intention was to widen their market appeal, targeting the combination of power and luxury that had once been the sole prerogative of Mercedes and BMW. To pay more than lip service to the public's safety wishes and his masters' quality and luxury wishes, Schäfer chose to increase the size of the body once more. The less than kind-hearted described his actions as one of 'bloating' the car. To retain the look of previous Golfs, he relied on even larger C pillars, and in an age when glass ruled the roost, with many cars featuring a third panel of glass down each side and the slimmest of C pillars, was mercilessly criticised for it. Safety considerations added weight. Quality and luxury likewise went hand-in-hand with a double chin and increased waistline! The chart below illustrates succinctly what had happened, while also introducing the reason behind the less keen and mean look, so much a part of the GTi's make-up previously, if not necessarily all other models.

Mk 3 GTi 16-Valve vs Mk 3 VR6 at launch and Mk 2 GTi 16-Valve late production

	Mk 2 GTi 16-Valve	Mk 3 GTi 16-Valve	VR6
Weights and Measures			
Length mm	3,985	4,020	4,020
Width mm	1,680	1,710	1,710
Height mm	1,405	1,405	1,405
Wheelbase mm	2,475	2,475	2,475
Track front/rear mm	1,432 / 1,429	1,450/1,434	1,450/1,434
Gross vehicle weight kg	1,413	1,645	1,680
Engine			
Cubic Capacity ltrs/cc	1.8 / 1,781	2.0 / 1,984	2.8 / 2,792
Bore/Stroke mm	81 / 86.4	82.5 / 92.8	81 / 90.3
Max output PS at rpm	139 / 6,100	150 / 6,000	174 at 5,800
Max torque Nm at rpm	168 / 4,600	185 / 4,400	235 / 4,200
Compression ratio	10.0:1	10.5	10.0
Wheels and Tyres			
Wheel Size	6J × 14	6½J × 15	6½J × 15
Tyre Size	185/60VR 14	205/50R 15V	205/50R 15V
Performance			
Top Speed	129	134	140
Acceleration in Seconds	7.9	8.7	7.6

Most notable when comparing like-for-like models was the increase in weight between the Mk 3 and its predecessor, a sum total of 232 kg – assuming VW's figures have been correctly transposed from the design department to the sales brochures. In layman's terms that's the equivalent of nine-plus 25 kg bags of potatoes.

With that burdensome extra weight there was an opportunity to roll around corners – GTis and the VR6 were gifted what was called 'Plus' front suspension, which improved steering under power, but there was no attempt to add the rear anti-roll bar bestowed on the crème de la crème to the spec of lesser offerings.

VW's market research implied that safety, if not the more formal addition of health, was steadily climbing the ladder in terms of customer priorities. When the Mk 3 finally hit the showrooms, as if to prove a point, the UK's twenty-four-page launch brochure devoted four pages to the subject in both written and picture form. Schäfer's design ensured the Mk 3 passed tough US safety legislation tests, where a sacrifice car could be driven into a concrete wall at a minimum of 33.5 mph without detriment to the driver and passengers. To achieve this feat, and make the car 30 per cent sturdier than its predecessor, demanded the sills and central door pillars were strengthened and the doors reinforced. A suitably rigid cross-member was to be found behind the dash, while another was located under the front seats. Further measures including anti-submarine effect seats and rear-seat backrests with a sheet-metal back, made the car ultra-safe but groan under its own weight.

Enter a new type of Golf with an inline V engine

The need to accommodate a package assisted Schäfer in the fulfilment of a key demand. He was requested to produce a shell that looked generous in its external appearance and an interior space that could accommodate five double chins and expanded waistlines with ease; a body that would ease the Golf – if suitably wrapped up with a big engine such as a VR6, V standing for Vee and R for Reihenmotor, literally Vee inline engine – into the path of the oncoming luxury brands of BMW and Mercedes models. Volkswagen's determination to add another dimension to the Golf's appeal also meant a car with more power, but a different kind of power, than the fastest of the Golf's, the initially absent Mk 3 16-valve GTi. Why exactly the 16-Valve GTi wasn't launched at the same time as its sibling 8-Valve model is a matter of speculation, although to suggest it was held back to encourage sales of the newbie VR6, as some have, is erroneous. The GTi 16-valve was finally launched in January 1993 and there was ample room in the showrooms for both models.

Few who purchase a Rolls-Royce do so for the 0–60 mph time it offers, or the off-the-scales maximum speed it is capable of pumping out. Instead, luxurious comfort is invariably the primary consideration. Volkswagen's VR6 engine was likewise developed to offer the inherently smooth drive characteristics of all genuine limousines. A GTI owner and particularly a 16-valve driver might well head off to the racetrack, while the VR6 was designed to attend a society gathering.

Schäfer's 30 mm wider stance for the Mk3 Golf, coupled to increases in both front and rear track, plus varying offset wheels which meant they were flush with the bodywork whatever their size, helped to give the impression of a more substantial car – ideal for the VR6, perhaps not quite so appealing as far as the GTi image went, and frankly ridiculous

'The VR6 combines the advantages of an in-line six cylinder engine with those of the 60 or 90 degree "V" design being both short and narrow.'

From cutaway drawings at the VR6's launch, to little more than a filler image. Nevertheless what stories pictures couldn't relay – words such as 'luxury' and 'effortless performance' – helped to tell the VR6's tale.

Partway through the VR6's Mk 3 incarnation Volkswagen's marketeers saw great benefit in moody, atmospheric photography – invariably with a black car taking centre stage. Filters further suggested the mystical, exclusive nature of VW's flagship Golf.

While the rear lenses of the VR6 might be dark by design, there was no need to obscure much of the car in the gloom of a star-free night – or was there? The VR6 badge stands out to great effect.

In reality quite appealing if slightly sombre, the interior of the VR6 looks more like that of a seedy, ill-lit nightclub.

for the base model Golfs with little under the engine lid and few of life's luxuries apparent on opening any door.

On the other hand, recall what *Autocar* and *Motor* magazine had to say for themselves in February 1992. Now take of note what they added. 'On the other hand, a feeling of maturity and deep-down build integrity has arrived. For a high volume family hatch, it's profoundly impressive.' Specific to the VR6 in straight competition with the BMW 325i, the fact that such a beast was chosen by *Autocar* and *Motor* as a direct threat would have had VW whooping with joy. The verdict was unequivocal.

> This is a car which lives up to its lofty aspirations to a degree that we could scarcely have imagined... The Golf VR6 is faster, more economical, more fun to drive..., more refined in several key ways... It is easier to drive fast or slow, it has more room inside, a heap more day-to-day practicality and an engine that's just as characterful... The VR6 is indeed the first of a new breed.

The VR6 could boast seventy-seven meaningful exterior or interior attributes to its name; the once splendiferous GL a mere sixty-one; and the 16-valve GTi no more than sixty-eight. While a full leather interior was still an extra cost option, at least it was on the list and could be added into special edition specifications with ease.

However, as the auto-journalists concluded in their numerous reports, it was the six-cylinder engine, and not trimmings and the bigger car look, which made the VR6 the flagship Golf of the range. Rather than opt for the traditional in-line configuration,

Left and below: Towards the end of production of the VR6 a 'Highline' version was offered. The exterior looked little different to the standard model, despite its special pearl effect Diamond Black or Purple Violet paint. However, inside appeared positively funereal thanks to the appearance of black leather. The other option, blackberry, was almost as dark.

VW developed a 'V' formation for the cylinder block, making for a much shorter and considerably narrower unit than the conventional V6. First offered with the Passat about six months before the Golf Mk 3's launch, the engine's secret was in the range availability of torque rather than sheer power. As the chart on page 61 indicated maximum torque of 235 Nm was achieved at 4,200 rpm, but a minimum of 201 Nm was available from 2,000 rpm across the board to 6,000 rpm. Quite simply, the car could rocket forward at a touch of the accelerator, but also glide along virtually without interference from the right foot - a true luxury cruiser.

The rest of the pack

After so many VR6 related words some might think the Mk 3 was a one-horse wonder, all other models stagnating in its shadow, but this was not the case. VW took steps to negate the weight factor and in general the engines offered notched up the cubic capacity as a result, but inevitably produced results similar, or even less impressive. Motoring journalists condemned the basic 1,400 petrol engine as underpowered for a car of the Golf's weight and proportions, but perhaps VW saw it as an about-town-and-no-more car, 0–62 mph times being of little importance in a Tesco car park. The unchanged 1,800 power plant linked to GL trim now limped to 62 mph in 14.2 seconds, whereas when slotted into the Mk 2 VW claimed a much beefier 9.8 seconds. Top speed was down a couple of notches too – although at 109 mph it wasn't that bad!

Associating the latest Golf GTi with the success story of its predecessors was sufficiently important that only an enticing section of the Mk 3 made it to the cover of the earlier GTi brochures.

Above: Without the GTi badge attached to the Mk 3's grille there was little to indicate that the latest in the series of hot hatches was indeed that kind of car. Gone was the indicative red trim lines and, thanks to the MK 3's more bloated look when compared to its predecessors, some thought that VW had designed a car for the middle class and middle-aged.

Left: The 16-valve, 2.0 litre, 150 PS engine for the Mk 3 GTi produced maximum torque of 180 Nm at 4,800 rpm.

With the Mk 3, had the fire of the hot hatch been extinguished? The contents list for the brochure from which this picture has been taken lists the following as its major topics: stylish driving enjoyment and comfort; all round quality both inside and out; active and passive safety; built-in safety; the Volkswagen airbag system; and environmental responsibility in design and manufacture.

Although the quality of materials used in the manufacture of the Mk 3's interior looks superior to those of earlier models, as with the VR6 the car appears gloomy, offering little to liven up the spirits.

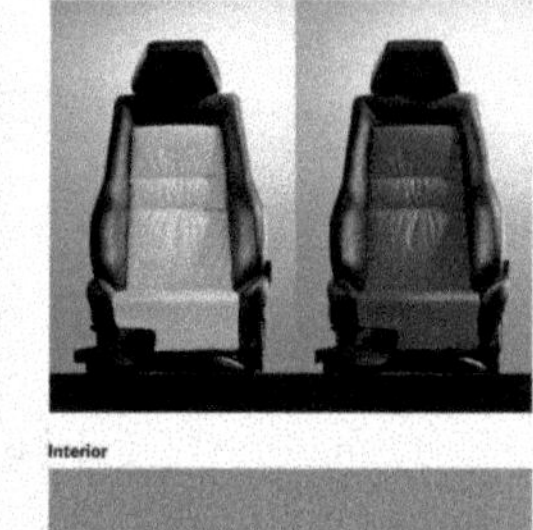

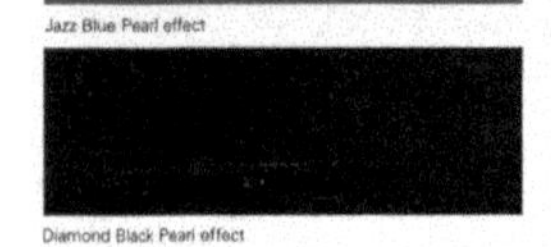

In 1995, amid a degree of sombreness not previously experienced with the GTi, up popped a limited edition of what were known as 'Colour Concept' Golfs. VW described the colours of their paintwork and the leather upholstery trim, which extended to the steering wheel and the gearlever gaiter, as 'vibrant'. Some bold individuals might have thought garish more appropriate. Other goodies at little or no cost boosted sales.

As for the GTi twins, both options sported a 2.0 litre engine – the 8-valve offering 115 PS and the 16-valve a lively 150 PS. Nevertheless the bodyweight still resulted in the 16-valve engine taking an extra second to achieve its target of 62 mph when compared with the MK 2 16-valve GTi's eager 8.7 seconds. Torque may have improved, but nevertheless the GTi in any guise came in for criticism – a problem to be laid at the door of the stylists who, latter day limited edition models excluded, had created a car that externally was virtually indistinguishable from the slowest of Golf tractors.

Banished from the line-up was Formel E as a marketing tool, the lack of enthusiasm for the cause being the reason; in the 1990s economy was expected of a top gear anyway. Fortunately there was something else for the fashion-followers to martyr themselves with, assuming they were happy to board the diesel-enthusiast bus.

Initially, British owners were lumbered with what was known as the Umwelt or 'environment' diesel. This equated to one of the first production diesels with a catalytic converter – in other words clean but slow, with acceleration from 0–62 mph taking 15.4 seconds. Compensation for some came in the form of engine flexibility. Fortunately, in 1993 a TDI was added to the agenda, an engine offering a 0–62 mph time of 12.8 seconds and a top speed of 110 mph. For those not impressed, the 90 PS engine pounded out 202 Nm at 1,900 rpm in terms of torque, comparing favourably to the 8-valve GTi's 166 Nm at 3,200 rpm. The route to diesel potency was finally on its way.

It should be added that 1993 saw the addition of the long overdue first estate car version of the Golf, though there had been both a Golf van and a pick-up for some time. The estate was well over 300 mm longer than the car and came with 40 per cent more load space. With the rear seats down, that equated to more than 1.41 cubic metres.

The Mk 3 also saw the arrival of a completely new Cabrio as the Mk 1 version, which suitably face-lifted had continued throughout the era of the Mk 2 hatch, was finally deemed to be past its sell-by date.

1996 saw production of a limited edition GTi known as the '20 Jahre Golf GTi' in Germany and the 'GTi Anniversary' in Britain. The trim package, for that is what it was, could be specified with either the 8-valve or the 16-valve engine. Apart from BBS alloys, red brake shoes, a large front spoiler, front fog lights and twin exhaust pipes (some of which were standard to regular GTis), the theme was 'racing red, what else?'

The GTi Anniversary featured red striped bumpers, black and red checked seat facings, red stitching to the leather covering of the steering wheel, gear lever and handbrake (including the release button), red seat belts, red bordering to the floor mats, red instrument needles with contrasting silver face to the dashboard dials, and red GTi badges front and rear. This package set the celebratory GTi apart from the rest.

The interior of the Gti Anniversary saw the return of an old favourite. However, the golf-ball gear lever was now crafted in aluminium, while the letters GTi on its top were highlighted in red.

During 1993 an estate version of the Golf was finally added to the list of available models, the task of carrying larger loads always previously having been the sole territory of the larger Passat.

One of the most unusual limited edition models was the 1995 Golf Rolling Stones. At the time Volkswagen had tied up with various bands. Available as either a three- or five-door model, the Rolling Stones edition came with the 1.6 litre 75 PS engine, not to mention a 1.8-litre Cabriolet version. Goodies added to the basic package included alloys and a top-class Sony CD player. Specific references to the Stones were more-or-less restricted to decals at the base of the C pillars and the addition of the band's name below the Golf badge at the rear.

1997–2003: Mk 4 – 'At the heart of every car is the engine'

With 4.83 million sales to its name and six years as VW's primary ambassador, the Mk 3 bowed out, making way for a car that was still recognisable as being a member of the Golf dynasty but, as the quickest of glances at the facts and figures shows, was once again heavier than its predecessor. Wasn't weight the factor with which numerous attempts had been made to tarnish the Mk 3's reputation? Yet all of a sudden piling on the kilos was no longer a defining issue. Why?

Designed in house, this time led by Hartmut Warkuβ, previously of Audi repute, many consider his Golf to be something of a 'timeless classic', elegant in every respect. For his part Warkuβ thought it made sense 'to underline the company's strategy in an evolutionary

Both larger and heavier than its predecessor, the Mk 4 Golf attracted little, if any, criticism in this respect. Its elegant styling appearing less chunky than that of the Mk 3.

If there was criticism to be levelled at the Mk 4 it was in the area of identity. Externally there was little other than badging to distinguish which model was which. Red cars these might be, which would have hidden red trim in the past, but VW had decided not to incorporate red trim into the Mk 4 GTi package.

rather than a revolutionary way.' Thus on a relatively minor scale the new-look, near oval headlight unit of the Mk 3 evolved into the eye-catchingly smooth affair that incorporated all aspects of the Mk 4's front lighting from single to twin headlights, plus indicator lamps, fog lights and so on. Of greater significance, the robust nature and solid proportions of the C pillars couldn't fail to impress, especially when linked to the low-line stance that had been missing from the body-kit look of the Mk 3.

With the Mk 4, the aspiration to produce a car to rival the products of Mercedes and BMW, achieved with the VR6 in Mk 3 days, had been extended through external aesthetics and internal design attributes – both factors that, due to their nature, couldn't be excluded from even the most basic of trim levels. The dashboard may have been made of plastic like those of all other manufacturers, but there was no hint of a hard and brittle finish synonymous with design to a budget. The controls were conservatively elegant, suggesting calm quality rather than the wild gimmickry of some others. While the seats in the most basic of Golfs still looked both inviting and comfortable, it was the little touches like twin cupholders at the front and in the rear in some instances, plus vanity mirrors incorporated into both sun visors, that made the difference.

So appealing was the Mk 4 that, when presented to the press in Bonn on 18 August 1997, few mentioned an increase in length of 129 mm, in width of 40 mm, and even in height of 14 mm despite that low profile. Similarly ignored were the fact the wheelbase had expanded by 36 mm (devoted to boot space and rear legroom), while front and rear track

Having noted that the alloy wheels shown in this early Mk 4 press shot were an extra cost option, the only way of distinguishing E, S and SE models from the luxury or performance cars was to note the black bumper and side mouldings. Higher up the ladder these would have been colour-coded.

had increased to 1,513 and 1,494 mm respectively. As for the key weight figure, comparing as near as possible like-for-like models, the Mk 4 GTi 1.8T and the Mk 3 16-valve GTi demonstrated a disparity in favour of the earlier car of 50 kilos, yet the press remained silent. Not that the Mk 4 got off totally scot-free, but the criticism levied was a little way down the road and was niche in its nature when it came.

Inevitably, production of RHD cars debuted later than those cars bound for LHD European roads. Similarly, not every conceivable trim and engine combination was set to grace British roads from May 1998. However, a flick through the pages of a British launch brochure – itself a much more extensive and glossy production than those of times past – unveils a further reason why the Mk 4 attracted maximum brownie points from many a journalist. Starting with the entry level E and its choice of a 1.4 litre, 75 PS petrol engine (borrowed from the Polo) and 1.9 litre diesel offering 68 PS, via the next-step-up-the-ladder S (add a 1.6 litre, 100 PS, petrol engine and a 1.9 litre 90 PS TDI, plus electric windows and central locking), the copywriters were soon extolling the virtues of an almost new engine and the desirability of adding a turbo to the GTi's specification.

Enter the V5 and the GTI 1.8T

No doubt to the surprise of many the onetime flagship VR6 wasn't anywhere to be seen. In its place was what VW opted to call a 'new type of luxury car' – the V5. The five-cylinder, narrow 'V' 150 PS engine was both smooth and powerful. Two-stage inlet manifold geometry

As the text confirms, the V5, here with the later 170 PS engine, was a luxury vehicle offering plenty of power and super-smooth performance. As the style of alloys depicted were an extra cost option, the only external distinguishing feature was the V5 badge attached to the grille.

Lift the lid and the V5's engine was shrouded in covers. Volkswagen reminded you of your car's capabilities with this V5 badge, which was only visible with the bonnet lifted.

Here is the V6 4MOTION, as can be confirmed by the grille badge. The glimpse of the interior seen through the windows might go some way to revealing that the car was far from a budget model.

ensured a high, flat torque curve that rose to 205 Nm at 3,200 rpm while maintaining 90 per cent of that maximum from 2,300 all the way up to 5,300 rpm. Acceleration from 0–62 mph was identical to that of the GTi 1.8T at 8.5 seconds and both had a top speed of 134 mph, although the style of driving by owners would undoubtedly have been different, the addition of an automatic V5 more-or-less confirming this.

The 16-valve GTi's replacement was, as has been loudly hinted, the GTi 1.8T, the 'T' standing for turbo. At last, mainly thanks to Audi, VW's engineers had accepted the notion of a petrol engine with a turbocharger. The five-valve-per-cylinder engine gave no sense of turbo lag, producing maximum torque between 1,750 and 4,600 rpm. Here was its big advantage over the 16-valve. The top speed of the two engines was the same, although the 1.8T was marginally faster in the 0–62 sprint (8.5 vs 8.7 seconds).

Invisible Golfs, a fake GTI and a diesel revolution

In among such goodies – for British drivers at least – were two potential reasons for journalistic malcontent. First, in addition to the turbo-charged GTi, Volkswagen in the

Middle-of-the-road SE trim levels indicate just how far Volkswagen was determined to go in pursuit of luxury. Note that owners could specify lower trim panels to match their upholstery and the chromed quality of the automatic's drive position selector and surround.

People had mixed feelings about Volkswagen's walnut trim package, standard with the V6 4MOTION and the Sport specification of the booted Mk 4, the Bora. The six-CD auto-changer and electronic climate control are indicative of the luxury package associated with such models. Leather upholstery, not shown here, was increasingly commonplace.

UK offered what was known as the Highline in Germany (essentially a trim level) and marketed it as a GTi. Externally, apart from smaller wheels – 15 rather than the 16-inch Montreal alloys bestowed on the GTi 1.8T – and a badge on the hatch proclaiming 'GTi' in chromed letters rather than the 1.8T's red 'I', there was nothing to distinguish the two cars. Inside and under the bonnet was a different story, the all-chrome badge GTi presenting a reasonably luxurious face inside, compared to the more sporty and GTi-like interior of the red 'I' turbo-charged package that included Recaro sports seats and black wood inserts. And, of course, under the bonnet the lowlier GTi lacked a turbo-charger. Initially the Highline was powered by a five-valve per cylinder 1.8 litre engine that offered a top speed of 125 mph and 0–62 mph of 9.9 seconds. In 1999 this was replaced by a 2.0 litre offering that had the effect of reducing the top speed to 121 mph and holding back the magic 0–62 sprint to 10.5 seconds. This GTi wasn't a GTi at all!

The other niggle was voiced not just in the UK. As the lowliest of the low Golfs were now endowed with colour-coded bumpers, and admittedly a black trim rather a colour-coded insert up to and including SE trim level, such humble beasts were almost indistinguishable from their ennobled siblings; the status of posh Golf ownership was therefore devalued. Add this at GTi level with the ongoing absence of such distinguishing marks as red grille piping, side markers and darkened tail light clusters, and there was discontent in the hot hatch camp.

Fortunately hope was not lost, as in 2002 a special GTi 25th Anniversary model went some way to restore hot individuality. 'Outside, unique shaped bumpers and widened sills are complemented by 18" BBS alloys', declared the press release, 'while a roof spoiler, 90 mm chrome exhaust and distinctive GTi badging ... complete the look.'

More significant, however, was a new to the Golf 1.8-litre, 180 PS engine that, mated as it was to a six-gear box, pumped out a top speed of 138 mph and covered the 0–62 mph sprint in just 7.9 seconds. This engine, alongside the faithful 150 PS engine it partially displaced, would remain a standard part of the engine roll-call to the end of the Mk 4 days.

Also a part of the Anniversary line up was a superfast diesel, which offered 150 PS, although this power offering had actually been launched towards the end of 2001. Driven by governments and lobby group initiatives far and wide to abandon petrol in favour of diesel, VW were eager to improve the performance of this kind of car. First came the 1.9 litre 130 PS TDI PD, soon to be followed by the 100 PS TDI PD and the seriously threatening 150 PS TDI PD. The key to such ratings lay in the initials PD. Standing for Pumpe Düse (Unit Injector), PD described a fuel injection system that could operate at pressures of up to 2,050 bars, much more than common rail systems when applied to engines of under 2 litres. Higher injection pressures meant better mixing of fuel and air.

The chart on page 87 summarises Golf diesel performance and the reason why such cars became so popular.

Above and left: The GTi 25th Anniversary Edition went some way to addressing the Mk 4's identity issues. Features of the car (that was limited in Britain to just 1,800 numbered examples) included the exclusive front and rear bumpers, red brake callipers, widened sills, 'Recaro' sports seats in black with red detailing, race inspired aluminium pedals, black leather trim with contrasting red stitching around the steering wheel, gear lever gaiter and so on and so forth.

GTI
Golf

Previous page and above: Of greater significance was the new 180 PS performance engine mated to six gears and acknowledgement that a diesel GTi could rub shoulders with the petrol offering. The diesel Anniversary model was allocated the TDI PD 150 PS engine.

VW News Release, 18 September 2002. 'Motor sport history was made at Thruxton last weekend with the first-ever British race victory by a diesel car, in the shape of the Golf TDI.' 'Volkswagen leads the way in diesel technology.' Drivers were encouraged to join the bandwagon of high performance with excellent fuel economy.

The Diesel Revolution and Tell Tale Badging				
	1.9 litre SDI 68 PS (The traditional tractor-like diesel)	**1.9 litre TD 100 PS PD**	**1.9 litre TD 130 PS PD**	**1.9 litre TD 150 PS PD**
Badging		Chrome 'TD' Red 'I'	Chrome 'T' Red 'DI'	Red 'TDI'
Top Speed	99 mph	117 mph	127 mph	134 mph
0-62mph	17.2 seconds	11.3 seconds	9.6 seconds	8.6 seconds
Max Torque	133 Nm at 2,200–2,600 rpm	240 Nm at 1,800 rpm	310 Nm at 1,900 rpm	320 Nm at 1,900 rpm

Return of the V6: a boost for the V5

Meanwhile, VW hadn't been entirely idle when it came to petrol fuelled models with a new task for an old acquaintance and more power for the flagship models.

First, in May 2000 British customers could order a V6 – the old term of VR6 being simplified for the occasion. Press releases wrote of 'the most performance orientated of any Volkswagen yet introduced'. On more than paper this was indeed true. The car sported a 24-valve, 2.8-litre, 204 PS V6 engine, which was mated to a six-speed gearbox, but also featured 4MOTION (always depicted in capitals). At the time brand new, 4MOTION was a permanent four-wheel-drive system that employed a Haldex coupling. This ensured that the power of the V6 engine was distributed between front and rear wheels according to available traction. Off-road capabilities suggested the role the V6 4MOTION was to play, being awarded tow car of the year. In many ways the car's top speed of 146 mph and the 0–62 scramble time of 7.1 seconds were academic.

From 1 December 2000 British customers could take delivery of a revised V5 that demonstrated a 10 per cent increase in torque and a power hike from 150 PS to 170 PS thanks to the introduction of multivalve technology. Five cylinders with four valves each equated to twenty in total. Volkswagen decreed that their already smooth engine could now rev more freely and performed even better higher up the rev range. The car's top speed was now 139 mph, up from 134, while 0–62 times were cut from 8.5 seconds to 8.2. Maximum torque of 205 Nm at 3,300 rpm with the 150 PS engine increased to 220 Nm at 3,200 rpm.

As for the turbocharged GTi, here's a reminder that following the Anniversary model's appearance the 180 PS engine it boasted became a regular GTi option. A quick reference chart illustrates the differences between the two turbo-charged GTis now available.

Turbo-charged 20-Valve GTi models		
	GTi 1.8T 20V 150 PS	**GTI 1.8T 20V 180 PS**
Number of valves	Five per cylinder	Five per cylinder
Cubic capacity	1.8 – 1,781	1.8 – 1,781
Bore / stroke - mm	81.0/86.4	81.0/86.4
Maximum output PS at rpm	150 at 5,700	180 at 5,500
Maximum torque Nm at rpm	210 between 1,750 and 4,600	235 at 1,950
Compression ratio	9.3:1	9.5:1
Gearbox	Five-speed manual	Six-speed manual
Top Speed - mph	134	138
Acceleration, secs 0–62 mph	8.5	7.9

A late but very welcome entry

No wonder the marketing men spun the line that 'at the heart of every car is the engine' and in November 2001 at Essen, despite the relatively short time before the arrival of the Mk 5 Golf, there was to be one more humdinger of a Golf – a car known as the R32 for very good reason. Theoretically nothing more than a concept, the response to this Mk 4 like no other was overwhelming. Six months later the car was officially launched at Madrid.

R32
WOB R 32

Previous page and above and left:
The Mk 4 crowning glory – the R32. It offered immense power from its 240 PS V6 engine, six-speed versatility, and 4MOTION stability, combined with sporty looks that guaranteed everyone knew your purchase was no ordinary Golf.

The chromed R32 badge – incorporating stylised segments of a chequered flag bonded to an italicised 'R', the symbol of Volkswagen Racing (previously Volkswagen Motorsport), followed by '32' indicative of the 3.2 litre engine – appeared on both the front and back of the car. Answering criticism regarding the anonymity of the GTi and others, R32 reminders were also to be seen on the widened sills, both the front and rear floor-mats, the leather-trimmed steering wheel and the aluminium clutch, brake and accelerator pedals. Lacking the '32 element, the Konig sports seats, cloth or optional black leather, were embroidered with the other elements of VW's hot branding. Finally, lift the bonnet and R32 was emblazoned on the engine cover.

Was such a plastering of R32 symbols really necessary? Even a glance at the R32's external appearance told owners of lower ranking Golfs, not to mention keepers of cars from other manufacturers, that here was a special VW. Ready to pounce, the R32 sat 20 mm lower than lesser Golfs thanks to specially developed sports suspension, and sported a substantial honeycomb front air intake, a rear roof spoiler, and a unique rear valance designed to accommodate twin exhaust tailpipes – not to mention darkened rear lenses, special 7½J × 18 'Aristo' alloys with 225/40/ZR18 tyres open enough in their design to allow more than a glimpse of avant-garde blue painted brake callipers.

The question has to be, did people buy the R32 for the status associated with its appearance, or for what was under the bonnet? Certainly performance was to be envied as the R32's narrow-angle V6 spat out a top speed of 153 mph and was capable of completing the 0–62 mph challenge in just 6.6 seconds. While maximum output of 240 PS at 6,250 rpm was noteworthy, maximum torque of 320 Nm at just 2,800 rpm was sensational, allowing drivers to rattle through the car's six gears with alacrity. Further, the potential safety crisis of such a powerful engine being let loose with just two driving wheels was obviated by the addition of 4MOTION.

Such was the success of the R32 that the initial production target was increased and extended – even the number of paint colours available was lifted from three at the start to seven later! Manufacture continued after general Mk 4 sales were officially a thing of the past, making a useful if late contribution to the successful Mk 4 total of 4.99 million cars produced.

The Golf with a Boot

Production of the first Golf to sport a boot rather than a hatch began in August/September 1979 at Wolfsburg, some five years after the hatchback's debut. The official launch took place at the Frankfurt International Automobile Exhibition held in September 1979. That the booted car not only took so many years to emerge, but was so obviously a Golf with a boot welded on, reveals a great deal. The traditional three-box shape was falling out of favour in Europe as the ascendancy of versatile hatchbacks became increasingly apparent. The Golf with a boot might have been named the Jetta in an attempt to give it its own identity; it might have been designed by Giugiaro as well, but from the start it was very much an also-ran in Europe.

The second generation Jetta, still noticeably a Golf with a boot bolted to its rear, debuted in Europe in early 1984, but as a car perceived by ignorant Wolfsburg to be of second fiddle

At last a booted Golf that had its own identity and particularly so at the rear. The silver car is a Bora (Jetta in the USA) in V5 guise, while the gold car has the 'Sport' level of trim.

status, USA dealers didn't receive stock until 1985. The problem was that the American market wasn't so besotted by the hatchback concept. The Mk 2 Golf's US launch in September 1983 wasn't what the public wanted.

While third generation Golfs with a boot bound for America retained the Jetta name, European cars were branded as the Vento, in what appeared to be a deliberate attempt to dissociate the new model from its relatively poor-selling predecessors. In fairness to those taking such a decision, the Vento looked less like a Mk 3 Golf with rearward attachment. Nevertheless the name change did little to boost sales. European journalists weren't fooled and, adding tinder to the fire, even suggested the Vento was essentially boring. The third generation Jetta/Vento appeared in Europe in the first quarter of 1992, six months and more after the latest Golf. To the detriment of the American market, US cars didn't materialise until 1995 thanks to quality issues at the Puebla, Mexico, factory where stock for North America was built.

The failure of the name-change from Jetta to Vento in Europe to drive sales upwards led to a further rebranding exercise with the fourth generation model being given the name Bora. Production of the least Golf-like booted car so far began in late 1998 with a launch in the UK dating to the spring of the following year. Key to the Bora's individuality was the car's rear doors, which were not the same as those fitted to the Golf and its graceful curved roofline similar in style to that of the then-current Passat. A redesigned grille at the front and, more significantly, an aggressively near rectangular design for the front light clusters still didn't result in bountiful sales in Europe.

Despite the fuzziness surrounding some of the figures given in the Bora/Jetta vs Golf and Europe vs the USA sales chart, it is quickly apparent that the American market had a definite preference for a sedan, while the hatchback Golf had a firm grip on Europe. With the release of the fifth generation Jetta (the name being allocated to the booted small family car wherever it was sold), VW finally learned their lesson and launched the new model in the USA before any other market.

Although the oddity of a Bora Variant could be purchased in Germany and some European markets, the frontal styling of the Bora but lack of rearward sedan-like shape made it clear the car was primarily intended for the USA. It was launched at the 2001 Los Angeles Auto Show, and German examples were more upmarket than their Golf Variant siblings.

	Golf Sales Europe	**Bora Sales Europe**	**Jetta Sales USA**	**Golf Sales USA**
1999	703,932	97,805[1]	130,054[1]	23,456
2000	685,029	91,609	144,853	28,124
2001	664,328	73,228	145,221	31,271
2002	596,415	64,260	145,604	40,157
2003	494,832[2]	44,155	117,867	*29,342
2004		34,217	91,790	
2005		17,239[3]	104,063	

	Golf Sales Europe	Bora Sales Europe	Jetta Sales USA	Golf Sales USA
	[2] some Golf Mk 5 sales will be included	add 13,868 sales of the Mk 5 Jetta	[1] Production of the Bora/Jetta Mk 4 began in July 1999 - figure includes some Jetta Mk 5 numbers	* may include sales of the Mk 5 Golf

[1] Available space has precluded anything other than the briefest reference here to a Mk 4 version of the Golf Estate (1999) and what at first sight appeared to be a brand new Cabriolet (1998). In Germany you could purchase the Estate with either a Golf front end, or that of a Bora! As for the Mk 4 Cabriolet, this was pure Mk 3 technology dressed with panels that made it look like a Mk 4. The development of a brand new model was considered too expensive, just as it had been in the days following the launch of the Mk 2.

[2] Unless specifically referenced throughout, all dimensional, weight and performance statistics are drawn from Volkswagen and no other source. It should be stressed that in their various writings and brochures, on occasion the car giant quotes figures at variance with other official utterances. British market brochures often refer browsers to, for example, torque in lbs ft, and dimensions in inches. As a result, and for ease of understanding, such figures have been converted to the closest metric equivalent.

The style of the Mk 2 Jetta failed to convince would-be owners that it lacked Golf ancestry.

The third generation Golf with a boot was named the Vento in Europe but retained its Jetta title in the USA. In VR6 guise the car looked somewhat bloated but less like a Golf than previously.

Bibliography

Alder, Trevor (ed.), *VW Golf 1991–1994 includes VR6* (Ipswich: Transport Source Books, undated)

Clarke, R. M. (ed.), *VW Golf GTI 1976–1991* (Cobham: Brooklands Books, undated)

Copping, Richard, *VW Golf, Five Generations of Fun* (Dorchester: Veloce Publishing, 2006)

Copping, Richard (writing as James Richardson), *Volkswagen Golf GTI (*Ramsbury: The Crowood Press, 2008)

Hayes, Russell, *The Volkswagen Golf Story* (Wincanton: Behemoth Publishing, 2014)

Hutton, Ray (ed.), *Volkswagen Golf GTI – The Enthusiast's Companion* (Croydon: Motor Racing Publications, 1985)

Meredith, Laurence, *VW Golf* (Stroud: Sutton Publishing, 1999)

Pitt, Colin (ed.), *Volkswagen Golf GTI* (Hockley: Unique Motor Books, undated)

Ruppert, James, *VW Golf* (Ramsbury: The Crowood Press, 1996)